English for Diversity

English for Diversity

A polemic

by

PETER ABBS

HEINEMANN
LONDON

Heinemann Educational Books Ltd
LONDON EDINBURGH MELBOURNE TORONTO
JOHANNESBURG SINGAPORE IBADAN
AUCKLAND HONG KONG NAIROBI

SBN 435 80010 8

Published by
Heinemann Educational Books Ltd
48 Charles Street, London WIX 8AH
Printed in Great Britain by Cox & Wyman Ltd
London, Fakenham and Reading

Contents

		page
	Introduction	ix
1	Some Observations	1
2	A Change of Heart	9
3	The Influence of Social Class and the Mass Media	21
4	The Place of Literature	33
5	Creativity and the Teaching of English	49
	Epilogue	139
	References	145

Acknowledgements

Part 4 is based on a series of seminars on Creative Writing given at the Arts Centre, Bristol.

Some of the children's work in Part 5 has appeared in *English Broadsheets* or in the Teacher's Book to that course. The principles outlined in this section are more fully embodied in the course.

The poem 'The Truth Hurts Like The Fire Burns' by Yvonne Hinton has been previously published in the magazine *Help*.

The poem in two parts, 'Going to Church' by Judy Boulton has previously been read on the Epilogue (Southern Television) on 31st March 1969.

As industrialization has transformed the basis of social life . . . the schools . . . have thus been compelled to broaden their aims until it might now be said that they have to teach children *how to live*. This profound change in purpose has been accepted with a certain *unconscious reluctance*, and a consequent slowness of adaptation. The schools, feeling that what they can do best is the old familiar business of imparting knowledge, *have reached a high level of technique in that part of their functions, but have not clearly grasped its proper relation to the whole*.[1]

*For all the children I have taught
but particularly for those in my fifth-year English set 1968
whose work is represented in Part Five.*

Introduction

By our educational system we compel active children into passive adults. Numerous schools systematically (if unknowingly) destroy a living world of experience and substitute in its place an impressive, but dead, graveyard of facts. And why does this happen? It happens because we endeavour through education to preserve the *status quo* – and the *status quo* demands a certain sort of man: a man who strives after things, who is acquisitive and knows how to win: a man who is centred on Having not Being: who recognizes facts but is blind to experience.

It is true that before eleven in the nursery and primary schools, we allow the children their freedom. Education *really* begins in the secondary schools. Here the children are encouraged to discard their games and fantasies and – identities. They must now become serious. They must learn discipline, the ability to sit silently at a desk and take in the facts that the teachers give. In the evenings the facts must be memorized or applied to small problems which can be marked and assessed the next day. Of course, the facts are important, armed with them the children stand a chance of winning, of beating their opponents and gaining the teacher's and parents' approval. And finally – after five years – there are the objective examinations which will objectively inform the children whether they have passed or failed, won or lost. . . . But either way, it doesn't matter, because, at the top or bottom, *success or failure*, the schools have succeeded in breaking them in to the *status quo*. We have turned them from children into adults. The system has worked.

Is there an alternative? Can education be viewed as a force for social transformation? Can it be seen as a power which struggles to allow the full development of the person, not the person who conforms to society, but the person who conforms to himself?

If this were possible – how could it be achieved? It would involve keeping the child's experience alive and allowing it to extend and deepen. It would involve granting the children more freedom to work in relation with their own gifts and temperaments. It would involve room for much more mutuality – for working together as opposed to striving competitively – than the present system permits. And for this to be accomplished, a new school would have to be created.

The school would have to resemble more a creative workshop than a regimental centre and the staff would have to consist of men of imagination rather than men of dull and dubious scholarships.

This style of education would not need to justify itself with examination pass lists and files of statistics because the process would be understood as an end in itself – as an absolute which could *not* be defended by arguments outside of itself.

The purpose of this mode of education could be defined like this: education is the progressive movement of the child outwards into responsive relationships with the world and inwards into a greater understanding of himself.

It is the aim of this book to defend such a concept of education and to explore some of its implications. The first three parts are concerned with affirming the need for a greater concern with creativity, freedom and relationship in our secondary schools. The last two parts are concerned more specifically with suggesting ways of encouraging the growth of these human qualities in children, through the understanding of Literature and the teaching of English. I hope that the two parts, the theoretical and the practical, confirm and complement each other.

Finally I would like the pupils' writing to be considered the most important part of this book – for the writing demonstrates what the polemic can only assert. I would like to think, therefore, that the reader had at least considered carefully the quality and content of the pupils' work before making up his mind about the general arguments presented to him elsewhere.

PART ONE

Some Observations

'School metamorphoses the child, giving it the kind of self the school can manage, and then proceeds to minister to the self it has made.'[2]

One

'The first key to wisdom is assiduous and frequent questioning . . . For by doubting we come to inquiry, and by inquiry we come to the truth.'[3]
Peter Abelard. *(12th Century)*

It is eleven forty. There are five more minutes left before my weekly 'Use of English' lesson ends. I have spent forty frustrating minutes trying to get about twenty sixth-form boys and girls to talk. I have put the desks together to form a table and we all sit round it, the boys have chosen to huddle round one side, the girls round the other. Hardly anyone has spoken – except for me. Every question, every pause for comment, has been met with an embarrassed silence. Suddenly in the last few minutes, the lesson comes to life. In exasperation I have criticized them for their silence, for their passivity, for their dependence on me as teacher. The girls are angered by my remarks and speak up in self-defence. Although the boys do not speak, they nod their heads in approval.

This is the conversation, as I remember it, in the last few minutes of that lesson.

Pupil: What do you expect? We've been educated to shut up!

Teacher: How do you mean?

Pupil: Well, I mean we've always been asked to sit there and not answer back.

Pupil: It's rude to answer back.

Teacher: Why?

Pupil: That's what you're told isn't it? Because the teachers know their subject and it's their job to get it across to you.

Pupil: To pass the exams.

Pupil: That's it. And you don't know the stuff and they do – so you sit and listen.

Teacher: You find it difficult to speak openly to a teacher?

Pupil: Difficult!

Pupil: We're not used to it.

Pupil: We're afraid of disagreeing with you. You see it's daft – they expect us to change over-night when we come into the sixth form. They expect us suddenly to have views of our own. But you can't, just like that.

Pupil: We're used to sitting there and listening and we can't do anything else.

3

Pupil: We've been treated like kids.
Pupil: But you've got to learn this way because of exams.

Just before this 'Use of English' class I had listened to the following conversation in the staff-room about a typical G.C.E. question on river-courses:
'I do not believe that most rivers have such stages as youth, middle-age and maturity. If you look at a real river, you can't find them.'
'I agree, but all the same, the children must know it.'
'Why?'
'They must learn it because it's a question on the paper. And if they don't know it, you are responsible for your pupils failing the exam.'
'But the facts aren't even true.'
'Of course, it's stupid. But while we have examinations you have to knuckle down and do it.'

In another 'Use of English' lesson with a different group, I suggest that we do some imaginative writing. Some of the members of this group have taken English with me in their fourth and fifth years and are excited by the prospect. Others seem reluctant. It takes, however, two lessons of discussion before these pupils begin to express their opposition. This is how it was finally worded by one of the girls:

I took 'O' level literature, and for a whole year we did nothing but analyse, break apart, and study literature. Then, after the examination, the teacher said we could do some free writing – but you couldn't after that. After you've spent a whole year learning how to break things apart you can't say 'Right, let's forget it. Now start creating something yourself.'

Her attack made me, almost guiltily, remember my own method of teaching Literature with a fifth form. The premise of our lesson had been: 'honest reactions to Literature are of more value than received opinions'. One of the poems for study was Keats's 'Eve of St Agnes'. In open discussion, the majority of the class came to consider Keats's attitude to sex as unintentionally funny or as unhealthy. They also considered the movement of the poem to be blocked by the endless passages of description. At some point in the discussion, D. H. Lawrence was mentioned.
'Sir, can we mention him in the exam?'
'Why not?'
'They won't mind – if we mention Lady Chatterley's Lover?'
'I don't really know.'

'So it's a risk?'

'It depends on who marks it.'

How can one tell? How do I know if the person marking values honesty and personal response above academic tradition? I know at 'A' level, I was taught that Shakespeare put comic sketches in his tragedies to keep the dullards in the audience happy, and I also know of at least one 'A' level examiner who slashes points off whenever he reads this theory in an exam script.

In the 'O' level paper that my group had been studying for, the question on the 'Eve of St. Agnes' was phrased like this:

Give briefly the story of The Eve of St Agnes and illustrate how it gains from the way in which Keats has told it.[4]

So much for honest reactions being valued more than received opinion! But not all classes are working towards G.C.E. . . .

It is five past three. The third year, bottom stream, come down to the hall for their drama lesson. The hall is spacious and, except for a few chairs piled on either side, empty. Three boys romp on the floor. Two girls pull at the curtains which have been drawn across the large glass windows. Others kick their satchels across the floor and talk and shout and aimlessly nudge one another. One or two begin to put the chairs round in a careless circle. (These pupils are not considered 'good material'. They have been put together in the bottom stream. They are noisy, bored, disorganized.)

I stand and wait. These children are so pleased to be out of the cage of their class-room that they seem at first unaware of my presence. They continue to romp or to run between the curtains. Teachers passing by the hall obviously disapprove. Last year, under a different headmaster, drama was banned throughout the school. Drama, it was declared, was a *noisy* waste of time. A more common attitude in staff-rooms is that a certain amount of drama is all right for low streams, but that 'better' streams don't need it because they can get down to more important things – like preparation for G.C.E. examinations.

As I wait, two more members of the class come in, five minutes late. Have they had a quick drag in the lavatories? Characteristically, a number of boys in this class were caned last week for smoking. Gradually, in twos and threes the form moves to the circle of chairs – where I am standing. As they sit, they go on talking but more softly. Then —

'SSSSSHHH! He's waiting.'

'So what?'
'Let him.'
'So are we.'
'Shur-up.'
'Come on, le's start.'
'We're waitin' for him, ain't we?'
'Well shur your clapper then.'
'Okay! Okay!'

At last, the lesson is ready to begin. I talk about rows – rows they might have at home, how they arise, what people say, how reconciliations are possible. The class begins to join in the discussion, to argue with me and among themselves. Soon the form will be ready to divide into groups and go off to different parts of the hall to improvise on the situations we have been talking about.

I watch them as they choose their roles and begin to act out different scenes. Their work is crude – it lacks poise and confidence, but this is not really surprising when one considers the over-all nature of their education. Yet *they* are enjoying the activity, and, I suspect, gaining more than they ever could locked in their class-rooms smouldering under the many strategies used by teachers to keep on top.

When, as a student, I watched classes of the supposedly 'less able' being taken in secondary schools, I frequently heard the teachers throw out such comments as:

'Mr Abbs is here to see *how intelligent* you are.'
'I hope you show him *your best manners*.'
'We don't expect *much* but we do expect . . .'

Such remarks are clearly designed to break the confidence of the child in order to gain control over him. The remarks imply a lack, a lack of intelligence, a lack of manners which, if the pupil is submissively obedient, the teachers *may* be able to remedy.* The implication is that the child on his own standing, does not make the grade, is, in fact, in staff-room terminology, a 'thicky', a 'dud', 'one of the dregs'.

Not all children can see through such strategies – but a few can. Here, for example, if a very perceptive account of a repressive school by a fifteen-year-old girl:

I once attended a school in which education lay entirely in books. We had to learn whole pages of text off by heart in history and geography. All that

* They also reveal the two main preoccupations of secondary school teachers, I.Q. and manners.

seemed to matter in Chemistry was getting neat diagrams. I never heard a
note of music during Music lessons – all we learned was how to write music,
how many beats in a bar and so on. Even in Art we had to make sure all the
time that nothing got splashed with paint (we had to wear overalls) and there
was no such thing as self-expression. In this school there was no room for it.
In English, we learned poems off by heart and while reading a book, we had
to look up all the words we didn't know and write them down, so literature
was (almost!) killed for me. And to top it all, if you got a good mark, you got
a commend and if you got a bad one, you had a careless mark. If it was really
bad then you got a disorder mark and if you got two of those in a week, you
had to go and tell the Head in front of the whole assembly. Thus the aim of
the pupils was to please the teachers and get commends. The teachers were
robots and we had nothing to do with them outside the class-room.

The pupils were quiet, shy and with no individualism. They never ques-
tioned a teacher's opinion on something as the teacher's word was law.
School rules were so strict it was ridiculous.

But occasionally they could not stand the suppression. They would lash out
by for example, writing shocking things on the toilet walls. Frequently a
pupil cried in class under the teacher's glaring eye. At this school I felt I could
not breathe.

However, in my present school the freedom has given me a chance for self-
discovery. I am taught to conform but not forced to. I still have room for
self-expression and have a great deal of freedom . . .

The essay was handed in with a number of others on education. I
would like to conclude this chapter by quoting excerpts from them for
they suggest a way out of the oppressive atmosphere which stifles so
many of our secondary schools. I ought to point out that the essays
were written after one and a half years of 'open' English teaching.

Education to me should be exploration. Exploration of the child's mind into
subjects which interest and fascinate him. No child should be forced into
studying a subject which he finds dull because this will produce boredom, and
the child's mind will become lazy and sluggish losing all spontaneity and
enthusiasm.

The ideal education allows freedom of choice, and exploration only into
subjects which interest the child. This will encourage a will to learn and a
strong, natural character. . . .

Perhaps schools should be abandoned altogether, and each child be allowed
to explore life and educate himself in his own choice of subjects, but I've got
a sneaky feeling that most children would prefer to play than to learn, and
perhaps they should be allowed to do so, learning only when their interest
in education has developed sufficiently.

. . . In this respect education is half-way there, in reaching the perfect education. Education is still thought of as getting enough passes to get a good job. Most teachers are still interested in just getting the pupils a good grade in exams and there it finishes.

Before setting out to give my views on an ideal education, I feel it is only logical to firstly define education. The *New English Dictionary* defines it as 'The process of systematic training and development of the intellectual and moral faculties'. However, in my view I think this is too harsh and crude a definition. It indeed suggests that the person who is being educated is treated more as an object which has to undergo a number of processes, than a human being.

Education should not in fact suppress people as much as it does but give them greater freedom. Then I think if they were not forced to do anything they would work harder.

Every single subject whether major or minor is vastly important and should be available for anyone to learn. The curiosity which burns in a child when he asks 'Mummy where did I come from?' also burns in older people whether they know it or not, and they must learn. To some people the geometry of an object gives immense pleasure and they understand more about that object and the world for knowing about it.

The beauty of art and music makes life worth living for some people and for others the history of an idea or invention doubles its beauty.

Aside from that, it is pleasant to know why a ship floats for instance and why the moon waxes and wanes, instead of just dumbly acknowledging that it does.

The educational system of the world does leave much to be desired but it is, in my opinion, almost as good as it will ever become.

Conformity is a powerful word amongst the human race. From the time a child can talk onwards, he is continually being suppressed – being moulded into the ordinary everyday monotony of a non-thinking community; this being the right and proper way to exist in it . . .

At the moment people are so-called educated in masses. Everyone is expected to do the same, react the same and think the same. I feel that in order to educate a person properly, that person should first be treated as an individual.

PART TWO

A Change of Heart

In the midst of all our exultation over the achievements of the age ...
there sounds a note of poorly conceived contempt for the individual
man; in the midst of the self-importance of the contemporary generation there is revealed a sense of despair over being human. Everything
must attach itself so as to be a part of some movement; men are
determined to lose themselves in the totality of things, in world-
history, fascinated and deceived by a magic witchery; no one wants to
be an individual human being.[5]

One

'From the time a child can talk onwards, he is continually being suppressed – being moulded into the ordinary everyday monotony of a non-thinking community: this being the right and proper way to exist.'

Teachers, men and women who purport to be qualified in the art of guiding and informing – more than parents – can so often be held responsible for creating an environment of suppression and monotony. Why do they do it? What is their reason for restricting the range of the child's curiosity, for damming up his energies? One argument is invariably brought forward: education, it is said, exists for examinations, and examinations exist for the efficient productivity of the economy. An editorial in *Primary Education* has stated the position clearly enough:

> the development of necessary industrial qualities is our job. It is too late when youngsters enter work. It is too late when youngsters move to secondary schools. A lifetime of work habits has to be instilled whilst children are of primary school age.[6]

This was written in 1965. It is arguable whether it still holds true for most primary schools. I think that we now allow the child up to eleven a great deal of freedom to explore and extend his own experience and that suddenly, in the secondary school, we undermine that experience and put in its place 'serious' subjects.

However, the editorial does attempt a definition of the teacher's role – to develop in the pupil industrial qualities, and instil work habits. It is presupposed that, left to himself, the child would do nothing – the habit of work has to be drummed in. Education – according to this popular argument – is the technique of imposing certain desirable habits and attitudes on to the child. But *which* are the desirable attitudes? John Vaizey in a recent paperback *Britain in the Sixties: Education for Tomorrow* has made it clear to the teachers. First he puts forward the qualities that are out of date, and then those that are in demand:

> The schools which bear the greatest prestige in our system, and to a certain extent, the Universities of Oxbridge, have been concerned in the past with developing certain traditions of leadership which are extremely inappropriate in the modern world. These traditions were in a large part a response to nineteenth-century society when England had a vast overseas empire, when

the balance of world economics was in her favour, and when personal independence and initiative were highly prized. This has now become outmoded
by the realities of twentieth-century economics where detailed knowledge,
research, technical flair, and a clear recognition of the toughness of competition, are of greater value.[7]

The argument is not difficult to follow. Our economy – to prosper –
needs qualities A, B and C and not X, Y and Z. Therefore education
should produce A, B and C and not X, Y and Z. Our economy does
not want men who have a sense of personal independence – perhaps
they would not be persuaded into buying goods they don't require,
which would lead to the rapid collapse of many profitable industries? –
but it does need men with flair and men who can survive the toughness
of competition.

At a recent speechday, it was publicly declared that the job of
secondary schools was to process the raw material that came in at
eleven. John Vaizey prescribes the formulae – what behavioural patterns the robots must have when they pour off the mass education layer
belt at sixteen: they must have detailed knowledge, flair and power to
survive competition.

This argument is so absurd that it is difficult to reason against it. The
economy, something created by man, something man can control, has
suddenly become master. More than a master, a god. Instead of the
economy being regulated by man for his own well-being – the
economy begins to regulate man. How can it be done? A created thing
determining a being? An object determining a subject? It is manifestly
absurd and yet it is the reality of our time. Education spends years in
indoctrinating the child to accept it. It is supported in this by the parents
and by the immense powers of persuasion exercised by the mass media.
Education, parents, the mass media, are working together to inculcate
the absurd truths of our competitive economy. Again and again in
discussion with teachers, one will hear the remark, 'It's a competitive
world. They may as well learn it here.' The constant presupposition is
that education is there to satisfy the demands of the economy.

A further point must be made. The argument that moves from the
economic to the moral involves the complete relativization of value. If
the economy demands such people – then education should produce
them. But what if the system demands a man who is seething with
hatred against the Jews, who is ready to see them exterminated, men,
women and children? Is it then right? Can such an argument be defended? You may object that Britain 1969 is not Germany 1939. And
this is true. But *what* is Britain 1969? The amount of severe mental

disturbance that has erupted in our society,* the number of people who annually attempt suicide, the drug taking, are all symptomatic of acute distress. Is it that people cannot bear too much *un*reality? Is it that for all our instillation of toughness and objectivity, the human being finds the burden too great? The final tragedy for those people who break down into themselves is that they are treated with the objective methods (drugs, electrical treatment, sleep treatment, surgery) of normal and alienated man.

Yet whatever Britain is like at the moment, the point remains: one cannot argue from the economic to the moral. Economic systems vary and the question has to be asked, 'Which economic system is most moral?' R. H. Tawney has put the problem well:

A combination of unity and diversity is possible only to a society which subordinates its activities to the principle of purpose. For what that principle offers is not merely a standard for determining the relations of different classes and groups of producers, but a scale of moral values. Above all, it assigns to economic activity itself its proper place as the servant, not the master, of society. The burden of our civilization is not merely as many suppose, that the product of industry is ill-distributed, or its conduct tyrannical, or its operation interrupted by embittered disagreements. It is that industry itself has come to hold a position of exclusive predominance among human interests, which no single interest, and least of all, the provision of the material means of existence, is fit to occupy.

Since the Renaissance, the commercial world has become more and more powerful, and, at the same time, less and less moral. This is because its activity has not been connected with any values beyond itself. If one educates man for himself rather than for the economy, the time will arrive when he will feel obliged to take over the great powers of technology (neither good nor evil in themselves) and direct them towards the liberation rather than the captivity of man. Today we are beginning to see the stirring of such a development among the more responsible student movements.

Here, our argument moves from man to education to the social system. And this is surely the right sequence? The question that must now be asked is – who is man? What must man be to be himself?

* 'A child born today stands a ten times greater chance of being admitted to a mental hospital than to a university.'[9]

Two

What is the nature of the human condition to which man belongs? This is, of course, an enormously complex question and would be impossible to circumscribe, the condition being in a continuous state of change. But are there fundamentals, qualities which constitute man's nature? It is important to be clear *how* one is speaking when one uses the word man. When I have said that education destroys man's experience, this is a shorthand way of saying education is destroying those experiences of man which make him specifically human, is destroying those aspects of his being which constitute the uniqueness of his nature. If a man is unaware of his freedom, if he is unaware of his creativity, if he is incapable of loving, then one can say that he *as man* does not exist. What then are the qualities which make man unique?

Man is the being who is self-aware. Like no other animal in nature, he is self-conscious. He suffers, he enjoys, and he knows.

This self-awareness cuts man off from the instinctual inevitability of nature. He can look forward, he can look backwards. He is aware of choices. Man is free. But what is he free for?

Man is able to ask the question What is Truth? What is meaning? He is the animal who can call his life into question. For, as he is able to look into the future, he knows he must die. And awareness of his own extinction torments him.

Yet, although he is aware of death and the many limitations imposed on him by nature – yet man is able to express and extend himself through his own powers of creativity. Through his imagination he is a god – he can recreate the world. He can turn inanimate nature into the shapes of his imagination, from formless waste he can create beauty.

But, perhaps above all these, is man's power to relate himself to others. He alone can say thou to another. He alone can love. It is this power which in many ways can answer the disturbing questions of man's existence and without which the other gifts of his nature cannot be sustained. The child who is not loved dies, some in the flesh, others in the spirit.

As I intend to say more about the nature of consciousness, and the use of freedom and imagination, in the last parts of the book, I wish to confine myself here to a fuller consideration of this essential quality of relationship. In doing so, I want to paraphrase the ideas of Martin Buber. He has commented so finely on this aspect of existence, that it seems almost inevitable for one to follow in his footsteps.

Buber distinguishes between two kinds of relationship: the 'I-thou' and the 'I-it'. Now, and this is the central point, Buber maintains that the relation signified by the combination 'I-thou' can only be spoken with the whole being.

Here is an example of an 'I-it' relationship:

> The observer is wholly content on fixing the observed man in his mind, on 'noting' him. He probes him and writes him up. That is, he is diligent to write up as many traits as possible. He lies in wait for them, that none may escape him. The object consists of traits, and it is known what lies behind each of them . . .[10]

Two points can be made about this relationship. The first is that the observer does not see the observed as he is. The observer knows absolutely nothing of the life of the person. Yet what he sees is one sort of truth – it belongs to the realms of objective, verifiable truth. Providing he is aware of this, no harm is done. The danger is, though, that the partial perspective is taken as the full vision.

The second point is this. The observer, to concentrate on the traits of the observed, leaves out his own subjectivity. And this is why Buber says the 'I-it' relation can never be spoken with the whole being. The observer, in his search for definite things about the observed, excludes all those aspects of his own existence which interfere with the process.

Such relationships are no doubt inevitable. But it is urgent that we recognize their limited nature and realize that to be a person, the other relationship of 'I-thou' is essential.

In contrast to the 'I-it' relationship, the 'I-thou' relationship gives a total and unverifiable truth of the other which can only be known through participation in it. The truth lies in what we have called the realm of being, not having. Whereas the first belongs to the category of objective truth, the second belongs to that of the subjective. Buber asks the question:

'What then, do we know of thou?'

and answers:

'Just everything. For we know nothing isolated about it any more.'

Such a relationship can only come into being when the self is no longer an observer, looking *at* the person, but a participator. To do this, one must give oneself, and this is Buber's point, 'the "I-thou" relationship can only be said with the whole being'. It means presenting oneself. What is known about the other in such a situation is not an object which can be verified. It is an invisible and mysterious knowledge *between* two persons.

However, the I-thou relationship is not constant. It is ever fleeting and cannot be determined. It continually falls into the I-it (alternatively there is no reason why the relationship of I-it cannot ascend into that of the I-thou). As soon as one wants to survey the relationship, as soon as one treats it as object, it dies. As soon as one abstracts feature X or quality Y from the person he ceases to be thou. For these are abstractions, lifted out from the unity of the experience.

Yet Buber maintains that it is through this evanescent relationship that we become persons:

'Through the thou a man becomes I.'

This remark can be taken to be true from the very moment of birth. It is through relationship that the child survives.

> In the human infant . . . the impulse to communication is his sole adaptation to the world into which he is born. Implicit and unconscious it may be, yet it is sufficient to constitute the mother–child relation as the basic form of human existence, as a personal mutuality, as a you and I with a common life . . . All this may be summed up by saying that the unit of personal existence is not the individual, but two persons in personal relation: and that we are persons, not by individual right, but in virtue of our relation to one another. The personal is constituted by personal relatedness. The unity of the personal is not the 'I' but the 'you and I'.[11]

These observations become disturbing when one realizes how evasively, how seldom, communication exists in our society. The whole impetus of our economy, as I have suggested, and as I hope to show later in the section on the mass media, moves man towards only the 'I-it' relationship. He must want things. He must buy things. He must measure things. He must see others as potential enemies. He must strive against them. He must beat them. The acquisitive society, acquisitive for things, the acquisitive school, acquisitive for facts, knows little of the invisible spirit which could exist between people. It is unaware of the possibility of building a community based on the power of man to say 'Thou'.

> Each of us is encased in an armour whose task is to ward off signs. Signs happen to us without respite, living means being addressed, we would need only to present ourselves and to perceive. But the risk is too dangerous for us, the soundless thunderings seem to threaten us with annihilation, and from generation to generation, we perfect the defence apparatus.[12]

Three

I hope I have given sufficient description to indicate the answer to the question 'Who is Man?' Man, I have claimed, is distinguished by certain powers, the powers of consciousness, the powers of choice, the powers of creativity, the powers of human relationship. These powers ontologically define man. They constitute what makes his being unique. Man not animal. At the moment, so destructive is our society, it is debatable whether man exists. Can he exist in the present set up?

Erich Fromm has put the problem like this:

> Our society is run by a managerial bureaucracy, by professional politicians; people are motivated by mass suggestion, their aim is producing more and consuming more, as purposes in themselves. All activities are subordinated to economic gods, means have become ends; man is an automaton – well fed, well clad, *but without any ultimate concern for that which is his peculiar human quality and function.* If man is to be able to love, he must be put in his supreme place.[13] (My italics.)

At the moment, our secondary system of education accurately reflects these failings of society. Let us ask these questions about contemporary education:

1. Does our educational system create the man who is aware of his freedom?
2. Does education create the man who is capable of honest introspection?
3. Does education create the man who understands himself?
4. Does education create the man who is imaginative, inventive, original?
5. Does education create the man who is capable of mutuality – of saying 'Thou' to another?

Who can answer 'yes' to even one of the questions? These are the qualities that surely distinguish man yet each quality seems conspicuously absent in most of our secondary schools. Not merely absent – systematically rejected. What our education achieves, through a strategy of constant persuasion, compulsion and threat – is to turn man inside-out, to make him an object to himself in a world of objects. The alternative is to educate man for himself, to bring alive all those various qualities that belong to his nature.

17

The child should be allowed to explore much more for himself. The child is naturally, energetically curious. We should let him be. It is through this insatiable instinct that man comes alive. The teacher's job is skilfully to provide situations where the child can discover about the world, about other people, about himself.

We need to destroy the old bad methods of passive instruction. The pupil sitting at a desk, writing the facts that are dictated by the teacher, has nothing to do with life. It is the most efficient way of killing the mind of the child.

We should emphasize the whole person. We must give equal status to imagination, feeling and thought. All vivid understanding demands the dynamic interplay of the differing areas of the psyche. To exclude one area is to distort the others.

We need to break the illusion of separate subjects. Education is about life. Life is a fabric of relationships – the child should grasp this through his experience. Subjects which break off areas of knowledge and set up as independent islands have deceptive powers. Traditional teaching of subjects – first lesson mathematics, second lesson French, third lesson R.I. – is death to the understanding and should go.

The child should be allowed more freedom. We must give him more responsible choices. He ought to begin to take on the burden of his freedom in the classroom. This can be encouraged gently by the teacher inside the teaching situation. Also parts of the week in the school timetable could be left open for the child to select an activity – or create it.*

The petty tyranny that goes on in so many of our schools at the moment needs to end for there is no good reason why children should be made to wear uniform or made to wear their hair short. The uniform is often an excuse to make teenage girls and boys experience themselves as more childish than they are. Children should be allowed to express themselves in the styles they wish – in accordance with their real age.

We need to encourage the child's instinct for communion. We should encourage him to mix freely with others, to work in an undertaking with others. In such activity he will quickly learn to feel for the other, to respect him, or at least to learn to live with him. The power to relate to others is more important and more needed today than the power to know.

The fierce competition engendered by marks, positioning, internal

* The practical changes in the timetable that such an approach would involve are indicated on page 141.

examinations, external examinations and streaming should be finished with, for the competitive system is bound to create children who experience themselves as failures. For each smug child at the top there is an insecure and hostile child at the bottom. Any system that is responsible for the creation of such emotions can only be considered inhuman. Today we need men who can heal the schizophrenic splits of the world, black/white, Communist/capitalist, not men who increase them.

We need teachers who are alive, who have insight and understanding, teachers the children can really trust so that they can come to believe in their own expressive powers and uniqueness. It is only with the delicate, but reliable, support of the teacher that the child can really explore into himself and the outside world, good as well as bad. It does not matter so much what teachers know – but it does matter *who* they are.

Einstein claimed:

> The fairest thing we can experience is the mysterious. It is the fundamental emotion which stands at the cradle of true art and true science. He who knows it not and can no longer wonder, no longer feel amazement, is as good as dead, a snuffed-out candle.[14]

Teachers should come to recognize it as their task to stimulate this emotion of wonder without which learning is useless and life empty.

In his autobiography Edwin Muir generalized about education from his own experience:

> This was the feeling which my first year school gave me, a feeling of being shut in some narrow, clean, wooden place; it must be known to everyone who has attended a school, and the volume of misery it has caused will not bear thinking about.[15]

It is time for a change of heart, for different methods, for a new understanding. A change in consciousness does not cost money nor does it need an Act of Parliament. A good school – as A. S. Neill[16] has demonstrated at Summerhill, Mr Stone[17] in Birmingham, Sybil Marshall[18] in Cambridgeshire and many others – depends more on the persons and activities than on the qualities of the building. Of course, better facilities, together with more spacious and flexible building would be an enormous help, but we can begin, if we must, without them. And perhaps we can best begin by putting an end to that volume of misery which schools in the past have too often been responsible for.

PART THREE

The Influence of Social Class and the Mass Media

'Long before a thermonuclear war can come about, we have had to lay waste our own sanity. We begin with the children. It is imperative to catch them in time. Without the most thorough and rapid brainwashing their dirty minds would see through our dirty tricks. Children are not yet fools, but we shall turn them into imbeciles like ourselves with high I.Q.'s if possible.'[19]

One

'The evening meal is a time when the family comes together and can talk.'

'What about?'

'About what they've been doing.'

'There's nothing to talk about.'

'You sit silently?'

'Good Lord – no! We have the telly on at meal times. We have the table near telly and we all sits round and watches it. It's something to look at.'

'I've got a room but I never work in it. Do my homework watching the telly. It helps you to concentrate.'

'You wouldn't know what to think would you. I mean if the television was off.'

'I hate it all quiet. It makes you feel lost. I mean all cut off like.'

These are extracts from conversations with bottom-stream fourth-year pupils in a large grammar school. A number of remarks have to be made. Firstly: bottom-stream children are working-class. Why this is so, I hope to show later. Secondly, the mass media talked about – particularly television – is seen as a power for *contact*. Thirdly the children don't appear to talk, converse, relate with their parents. These points are all connected: the third could be seen to account for the second – and the third and second together to account for the first. This is in fact the order in which I want to approach the working-class situation.

From the moment a child is born the class roles begin – the patterns are laid down. The working-class child is born into a home where the television is perpetually on; where there is little silence; where reality is noise and pictures. By the time he is three he will be an avid watcher of television. His 'bad' behaviour will be punished by missing a favourite programme. His 'good' behaviour will be rewarded by sitting up and watching a late programme. His fantasies and games will develop from his television programmes. He will demand Stingray weapons or dolls shaped like his heroes, Captain Scarlet, Thunderbird, Tommy Gun, Action Man. Other toys will not be presented to him nor, even at three, would he be interested in them. *His* games are the real ones – they mirror the reality, the reality brought to him by television.

I have said his behaviour is manipulated by the power of the television switch. Much more needs to be said about this. The child's mother and father do not explain to the child the reasons for not doing this or that. There is no such exchange as the following:

'Don't pull the cat's tail because you hurt it and *you* don't like being hurt do you?'[20]

What is *said* is unimportant in a working-class home. It is what is *done*.

'Don't pull it because I say so!' moves on to 'Don't keep pulling its tail or I'll bloody do you.'

Here the aim of the parent is solely to stop the act. If the child doesn't stop it then action must be taken. A smack across the head or no television. The language could almost take place in grunts for it only expresses emotion. The consequences of this restricted form of conversation are enormous. The child comes to believe nothing of any importance is ever transmitted in language. There are no reasons for right and wrong. There are only absolute rules which are enforced. There are rewards and punishments. There are sensations and actions. But there are no explanations.

What effect does this absence of sustained rational and imaginative communication have later on at school? Education is achieved almost totally through the medium of the spoken and written word. Its fundamental presupposition is that words convey the nature of the world, the why and wherefore of things. At what a disadvantage is the working-class child! *His* presupposition, coming from five years of experience with his mother and father, is that nothing important is ever conveyed in words. Again and again as a teacher, one will hear among the bottom streams such remarks as:

'We never talk about anything at home.'
'What's the use of talking?'
'What good does talking do anybody?'
'What can you say?'
'They don't know me at home.'

How is one to break down a conviction which is a perfect expression of their own home experience, their own deep attachments? How is one to break down the terrible class-role that has been unconsciously assimilated by these children? At the moment our educational system actively confirms the role of the working-class child. He is labelled 'thick', placed in a bottom stream, and teachers can't wait until the day he departs for the factories. The teacher's only anxiety is that he doesn't disrupt the brighter pupils and doesn't injure the school, break it up or get it a bad name. This was the Victorian attitude to the working class – and it is ours as well. Nothing has changed in essentials. The changes in the last hundred years in our society touch only externals. We have more money, we have more possessions, and we have the mass media, to lull us into 'reality'.

It has been claimed that the working class are warmer and more physical than other classes; they may not exchange so much verbally, but they exchange, directly, physically; the working class have an instinctive tenderness. This picture of the working class is the romance of the intellectuals. The general truth seems quite the reverse.[21] The working class are terrified by their own bodies. It is, as John and Elizabeth Newson have shown, often a scandal to the woman that she has breasts and to the man that he has a penis: something to be anxiously concealed from their children.

These common working-class inhibitions about the body can only serve to contract even further the world of the child. 'There are certain things you should know nothing about.' 'You mustn't ask questions.' 'Don't touch.' 'That's none of your business.'

Certain things must not be known. Certain questions must not be asked. Certain actions must not be done. But there are no reasons. Nothing happens through words. Where do things happen? On television, in comics, in pop music. There you can be switched on. The mass media can give you life. . . .

Two

Let us return to the children's conversations.

'You wouldn't know what to think, would you – I mean if the television was off?'

'I hate it all quiet. It makes you feel lost. I mean all cut off like.'

The working-class child, not surprisingly, comes to depend on the mass media. It's not just a matter of entertainment. It's a matter of confirmation and even, identification. The television is on when he eats, when he works, when he reads, when he talks; when it is not directly in the foreground of his experience, it is indirectly there as an essential background of noise and movement. How far this is true of our society as a whole, it would be difficult to determine. But it has been postulated* that if all mass media (television, radio, papers, comics, magazines, films, etc.) were stopped for a number of days there would be throughout society a mass outbreak of mental illness. So dependent have we become on the mass media to justify or embody our lives for us! Still, this identification is probably the strongest among the working classes. Since infancy the working-class child has had unfailing contact with the noise and messages of the mass media. The television is the permanent breast – always there, always soothing, reliable and undemanding. The child, the teenager, is not anxious to question, or see through, his source of consolation. He could only come to do this through language, through directed and informed discussion, and that is the very process he is incapable of believing in. The commercial world is adept at exploitation – and here it has the perfect market extending far into the future, for today's teenagers are the mothers and fathers of tomorrow.

Enough books have been written to demonstrate the nature of the trash presented to the teenager on the mass markets:[22] comics which offer dream worlds of love that reliably end in the close-up kiss, which scrupulously avoid conflict and problems, which exclude, on principle, 'real' experience, American pulp which advertises the splendours of war, the blond hero who conquers the Japanese devil, and all manner of novels written to Fleming's formula 'of sex and violence' – sensationalized sex, romanticized violence.

How does all this – coupled with the constant persuasion of advertising, pop music, television and Radio One – affect the child?

* Erich Fromm postulates this in the *Sane Society*. While he is writing about the American condition it would not seem rash to apply many of his observations to our own society which is in danger of coming to resemble a miniature America.

It is impossible to answer this fully – but the English teacher, from his angle, sees the constant effect of the mass media on creative work. Again and again free drama enacts a plot on last night's television: a mundane plot with stereotyped characters. In discussion and written work the effect is even more noticeable. Consider these passages written by second year working-class girls in a low stream of a modern comprehensive school:

I love long hair. I love 'T' boots on boys with tight denim jeans. Michael Tucker wears either a suit or tight denim jeans, cuban heeled boots, a fur collared suède jacket, and he has long dark hair in the style of Dave Davis out of the Kinks (mmm) Phil May out of the Pretty Things is Gear and Brian Jones is fabulous. Dave Davis and Roy Davis (brothers) out of the Kinks. I like Top rank some gearboys get down their. When the smoochy records are on (mmm).

I love a boy of this description – about 5′ 4″ with fair swooping hair over his eyes, 1½″ cuban heels and tight jeans with a jacket, open-necked shirt and a black jumper underneath his shirt. I also like boys with mod clothes and also a mod haircut.

To go out boys need to wear a suit but on a night-time tight jeans and T boots look great.

One can quickly discern how such girls are experiencing their first relationships with boys through the slick externalities of the commercial world. Here perhaps there is an element of wish fulfilment, an underlying innocence, but in a few years' time it will be experience, unchanged in any of the essentials. What is most disturbing is the complete absence of all qualities like courage, kindness, faithfulness in these relationships. A person *is* what he wears. Love is a meeting with a type, not an individual. And this is the message which the mass media continually inculcates into our children.

But, it may be objected, there is great choice of literature, music and television programmes in today's world. This is, of course, true. It is good to see so much excellent music and art available. There is nothing more abhorrent than the idea of art being the exclusive possession of a certain class, especially when that class tended to use it merely as a superfluous decoration or as a sophisticated means of evasion. But this is not the point. The mass media *do* offer choice – but only to those who have the power to discriminate, only to those who can think rationally, feel imaginatively. The person who is not fully educated is not fully free. And where can the working-class child hope to be educated?

Where can he hope to gain these qualities – qualities that are the right of all people? The working class child has been indoctrinated in another mode of life. He does what he has to do because of the social pressures around him. Ironically the school is one of these pressures – keeping him a barbarian – as we shall now see.

Three

A very common assumption is that the working-class child is less intelligent than his middle-class counterpart. There is no evidence for this. The only evidence there is shows that the working-class child is *made* less intelligent by the circumstances that surround his life. Intelligence, like any other faculty, needs nurturing. It needs to be presented with the means with which to discover and express itself. The means largely consist of words. The development of language is inextricably linked with the development of intelligence.

> I have forgotten the words I intended to say,
> and my thought, unembodied,
> returns to the realms of shadow.[23]

But perhaps even this remark doesn't do full justice to the power of language. Is it possible for a thought to exist without words? It is difficult to conceive of a thought existing *without* language. . . . Yet we have seen the limited area of verbal exchange that happens in the home of the working-class child. At five when the child begins primary school he is already marked out from middle-class children, by his lack of curiosity, by his lack of forthright speech. By the time he enters secondary school he is in a bottom stream. And is made to know himself as no good. He is told he might be good at work, but not learning. His role has been endorsed.

It is not only the streaming system which keeps him in his place. The educational system is in the hands of the middle class and the middle class have a deep love for appearances, good manners, good speech, good dress. These are seen as the pre-requisites for success. Good, of course, means conventional – as the middle class choose to interpret the word. The conventions of the working class are obviously different. The children will have different manners and different dress and speech habits. But these are not acceptable to the middle class. Again and again one will hear the staff-room condemnation of children for the clothes they wear, for the hairstyles they have, for the language they use. These children, it is claimed make bad material for schools. Pity they are in the schools, but as they are we must just keep them down. Keep them in their place at all costs.

Which social class does the school serve? Without doubt the middle class. We still have three classes in our society and different modes of education for each. The upper middle class are to be found in public schools, the middle class are to be found in top streams of the State schools and the working class in the bottom streams. The secondary school system is constructed to flatter those who have the passive virtues of manners and memory. At speech day, prizes are lined up for the succesful. The parents of the successful, formally invited, flock to the school. The losers are absent. The working-class children with their parents are watching the television.

It is a great pity to have to talk so much in these class terms for ideally, education should destroy the notion of class. The only class we all belong to is humanity. And education should nurture this truth. But as the situation is, one is forced to be aware of the great divisions, and social injustices, that still heave and cry out beneath the Welfare State. There is a need for a much greater social reconstruction than we have achieved so far. Education would have to play a decisive part in this. At the moment we are just concealing the truths under misleading slogans for comprehensive schools. Nothing fundamental changes when you strip off one label and stick on another.

Four

SUCCESS BEFORE SIX.[24] This was the title of a recent series of articles on education published in the *Sunday Times*. And the title gives the whole game away. Education for the middle class is not an end in itself: the middle class have no more love for the humanly fulfilled man than the working class. It is the pathway to social and economic power. This was put quite succinctly by a top-stream third-year boy:

Education varies from school to school - but a good education is a key to a successful job.

Or perhaps nearer to the bone:

An important fact is that if you want to be lazy when you are an adult, you will have to work hard at school when young.

The middle class are responsible for inserting into education a lamentable snobbery and a petty spirit. What you do must pay dividends and then it is justified. What is the use of art? What is the use of drama? All that matters is that the daughter or son chooses sensible subjects and can do well in them. Education equals success. And what an exciting headline 'Success before Six' must have been to thousands of *Sunday Times* readers! What more could you ask for - except perhaps, the material consequences of success.

Children from such homes are obviously heading for top streams. The system can flourish with those who want to get on. These children will be able to prove themselves in examinations and be the triumphant justification of the educational system.

The middle-class man appreciates the respectability and money that education can bring. He has no more understanding of what true education is than the working class. If he was told that education meant the complete unfolding of the human personality, he wouldn't understand what was being said.

Yet for all this *genuine* education is more readily possible with middle-class children. Why is this?

It is again, a question of language and a question of the mass media.

The middle class tend to employ an elaborate method of speech with their children. This method of talking involves the use of precise words, often abstract, linked in a logical order. Here is an example:

You can't play with your toys now because if you do we will be late for the party and we were asked to be there on time. Put your toys away now

31

because if you don't there will be no point in going to the party . . . Which do you want to do?

The differences between this and the working-class pattern of communication 'Do it . . . or else' are fundamental. In the middle-class speech, reasons are given to the child. He must act like this *because*. . . . Again (and I don't think this is untypical) at the end the child has a choice of determining his own action. He can if *he* prefers, play with his toys. The working-class order tends in the opposite direction. 'You do what I tell you.' The real point is this: the world to the middle-class child does make sense and he can learn about it through language. The child with this attitude towards life can be deeply influenced by arguments counter to those of his parents. He is open to imaginative and rational communication – a real type of education can begin.

Again, unlike his working-class contemporary – he doesn't have to depend so much for contact on the mass media. He *can* talk (if only in limited areas) with his parents. He *can* gain from school – he enjoys it there, for his ego is strongly affirmed by the educational system. After watching television he is more likely to discuss what he has seen, to realize, in discussion, other points of view. At a superficial level he has already begun the habit of discriminating, of liking this more than that, and being able to say why. It is not difficult for education to deepen his critical faculties.

I have said it is easier to encourage the middle-class child to break into himself, to make him realize the possibilities of his own nature. But, of course, this seldom happens. The middle class and the schools are allied in their determination to keep education concerned with respectability and the future pay packet. Alienation must be perpetuated at all costs. And on the whole they are quite successful – even before six.

PART FOUR

The Place of Literature

'The whole is greater than the part. And therefore, I, who am man alive, am greater than my soul, or spirit, or body, or mind, or consciousness, or anything else that is merely part of me. I am a man and alive. I am man alive, and as long as I can, I intend to go on being man alive.'[25]

One

'Today's child is growing up absurd because he lives in two worlds and neither of them inclines him to grow up. Growing up – that is our new work, and it is total. Mere instruction will not suffice.'[26]

The mass media and the school, in their own different ways work towards the same sort of person – the person who, desperate to acquire things outside of himself, loses himself. The working-class child is influenced more by the mass media. The middle-class child more by education. Different paths but the same destiny.

But how are we to incline the child to grow up in a *total* sense? In the second section I attempted to outline an alternative to the contemporary school: it was a school built up on the fundamental concept of man as man. Freedom, creativity, experience, relationship were insisted on. These qualities of being, I argued, were the inalienable right of all men for they were the marks of his nature. It was these qualities that made him man. If a society fails to embody them then the society must change, not the child. Man ought not to be determined by what is around him, but by *who* he is. If this means driving our horse and cart over the bones of the dead, then it must be done, for it is with man's possibilities that we are concerned, not with the museum of his past.

But there is much in the past that is not over. There are forces that are creative and dynamically alive, particularly in our literature. It is to a consideration of literature that I now want to turn. I intend to consider the importance of literature under these headings:

Chapter Two: That literature has for its aim the understanding of experience.

Chapter Three: That creation releases energy and frees the human personality.

Chapter Four: That the source of creation is often in disorder but that this is transcended in the positive act of creation.

Chapter Five: That meaning must inhere in literature because its medium is words: words with which we communicate both feeling and thought.

I use the word literature qualitatively. The amount of literature opposed to these principles is enormous and is fast coming to clutter, along with sweets and soap powders, nearly every shop counter in Britain. To counteract it, it is important to be sure in what the value of literature consists. Nor, unless we are fully aware of its value, will we be able to bring it alive in our schools, which will be my concern in the fifth part of the book.

Two

'Art is something subversive. Art and liberty like the fire of Prometheus are things one must steal to use against the established order.'[27]

One can only be amazed at how calmly the established order has tucked literature under its great wing. And amazed even further to see how snugly it fits there. Consider all the examinations in literature, 'O' level, 'A' level, Degree level. Consider the flock of literary critics who fill the English Departments of Universities. Consider the glut of learned theses churned out year after year, essay after essay on the significance of Eliot, the symbolism of Yeats, the primitivism of Lawrence. The least one could conclude is that literature has become both a respectable and a specialized activity of our society. What has happened to its subversive energy? For, indeed, literature does possess revolutionary power. More often than not literature is highly disturbing in its content, often having as its declared aim the systematic breaking down of any comfortable position. Great literature is an affirmation of madness in a sane world which has lost itself:

> Much madness is divinest sense
> To a discerning eye —
> Much sense the starkest madness.
> 'Tis the majority
> In this, as all, prevail.
> Assent and you are sane.
> Demur – you're straightway dangerous
> And handled with a chain.[28]

Perhaps we have succeeded in chaining our writers by that popular method, flattery at a distance. The threatening animals are confined in cages in our schools and universities to be admired. They really are rather fun to study. The subjective is turned into the objective – to the reduction of both.

The poet's approach is by its very nature subjective. His quest is that of penetrating and affirming life. There is no better way of demonstrating what I mean than to turn to the writing of creative men. Here is how Keats defined his vocation.

I compare human life to a large Mansion of Many Apartments, two of which

I can only describe, the doors of the rest being as yet shut upon me. The first we step into we call the infant or thoughtless Chamber, in which we remain as long as we do not think – We remain there a long while, and notwithstanding the doors of the second Chamber remain wide open, showing a bright appearance, we care not to hasten to it; but are at length imperceptibly impelled by the awakening of this thinking principle within us – we no sooner get into the second Chamber, which I shall call the Chamber of Maiden Thought, than we become intoxicated with the light and the atmosphere, we see nothing but pleasant wonders, and think of delaying there for ever in delight: However, among the effects this breathing is father of is that tremendous one of sharpening one's vision into the heart and nature of Man – of convincing one's nerves that the world is full of Misery and Heart-break, Pain, Sickness and oppression – whereby this Chamber of Maiden Thought becomes gradually darken'd and at the same time on all sides of it many doors are set open – but all dark – all leading to dark passages. We see not the balance of good and evil. We are in a Mist. *We* are now in that state – We feel the 'burden of the Mystery', to this Point was Wordsworth come, as far as I can conceive when he wrote *Tintern Abbey* and it seems to me that his genius is explorative of those dark Passages. Now if we live, and go on thinking, we too shall explore them. . . .[29]

Keats views youth as casually entering into the Chamber of Maiden Thought and suddenly becoming intoxicated with the delights and wonders that surround him. Then there is the sharpening of his vision into the heart and nature of man. Here, only pain, suffering, darkness can be discerned. Youth cannot turn away. He cannot quickly retreat back into the womb of peaceful sensations. He has to move forward, probe the darkness, feel the pain. Penetrating life involves penetrating both the joy and the suffering; the light and the darkness. Only this way allows experience to become whole, authentic.

It is startling to read Keats's letter alongside an essay by Herman Melville. Melville is writing about the genius of Hawthorne and the similarities of his comments with those of Keats's on Wordsworth must be seen as more than coincidental.

Where Hawthorne is known . . . he seems to be deemed . . . a man who means no meanings. But there is no man in whom humour and love developed in that high form called genius – no such man can exist without also possessing as the indispensable complement of these, a great deep intellect which drops down into the universe like a plummet. Or, love and humour are only the eyes through which such an intellect views this world. The great beauty in such a mind is but the product of its strength . . .

. . . For spite of all the Indian-summer sunlight on the hither side of Hawthorne's soul, the other side – like the dark half of the physical sphere – is shrouded in a blackness, ten times black. But this darkness ever gives more effect to the ever-moving dawn, that forever advances through it, and circumnavigates his world. . . . Certain it is, that this greater power of blackness in him derives its force from its appeals to that Calvinistic sense of Innate Depravity and Original Sin, from whose visitations, in some shape or other, no deeply thinking mind is always and wholly free. For in certain moods, no man can weigh this world, without throwing in something, somehow like Original Sin, to strike the uneven balance.

This black conceit pervades him through and through. You may be bewitched by his sunlight, transported by the bright gildings in the skies he builds over you, but there is the blackness of darkness beyond: and even his bright gildings but fringe and play upon the edges of thunder-clouds.

Now it is that blackness in Hawthorne – of which I have spoken – that so fixes and fascinates me . . . This blackness it is that furnishes the infinite obscure of his background – that background against which Shakespeare plays his grandest conceits, the things that have made for Shakespeare his loftiest but most circumscribed renown, as the profoundest of thinkers. For by philosophers Shakespeare is not adored as the great man of tragedy and comedy . . . – it is those deep faraway things in him: those occasional flashings-forth of the intuitive Truth in him: those short, quick probings at the very axis of reality: – these are the things that make Shakespeare Shakespeare. Through the mouths of the dark characters, Hamlet, Timon, Lear and Iago, he craftily says, or sometimes insinuates, the things which we feel to be so terrifically true that it were all but madness for any good man, in his own proper character, to utter, or even hint of them. Tormented into desperation, Lear the frantic King tears off the mask and speaks the sane madness of vital truth.

In this world of lies, Truth is forced to fly like a scared white dove into the woodlands: and only by cunning glimpses will she reveal herself, as in Shakespeare and other masters of the great Art of Telling the Truth – even though it be covertly and by snatches.[30]

Melville and Keats, so different as personalities and writers, are yet agreeing as to the nature of the poetic quest. They both sense the great darkness which surrounds the light. They both feel the need to express this in art, to explore it and to leave nothing out, however painful. Again they both sense that Truth, the penetration of life, is difficult for it entails taking on the oppression of the world. Art becomes the job of telling the truth – 'the sane madness of vital truth'. Melville's wording echoes Emily Dickinson's:

> Much madness is divinest sense
> To a discerning eye.

And how is one to arrive at this divine madness? Only through a daring

plunge into oneself. Again Melville phrases this vertical descent dramatically:

> I love all men who dive. Any fish can swim near the surface but it takes a
> great whale to go downstairs five miles or more.[31]

It is the job of educators at some point to provide the sea for that descent. The journey itself can only be conducted by the individual.

Art then is the attempt to break through to reality ('to raid the in-
articulate'), in order to circumscribe it, understand and affirm it. The
following poem, written by a fourteen-year-old, sums this up well:

Myself
I am very rare in my kind
    you may look but you will see nothing.
I am within myself . . . alone —
For I seek to find myself
    and to comprehend what I find.
I look for a way of living —
The purpose of life,
An excuse for dying —
Excuses . . . I have many.

The writer is already aware of his peculiarity – 'I am very rare in my
kind' – his is a solitary activity. Not one customary among his friends.
All the same, it need not be in any way a depressing or isolating experience. The very act of creation promises a fullness, quite closed to
those who look and see nothing. For all art is in love with energy.

Three

'The poet lives in gusto.' – Keats was in agreement with Blake's 'Energy is eternal delight'. It was through energy that one could become what one saw, know about it from the inside:

> If a sparrow come before my window I take part in its existence and pick about the gravel.[32]

Such a gift of empathy is perhaps rare. But need it be? We are so indoctrinated with a subject/object dichotomy, with the idea that 'I here' am learning facts about 'that over there', that it is more than possible this power of empathy is destroyed in us. Yet empathy, intuition, imagination, these are very real ways of knowing and give of their nature, a fuller reality than that offered by the objective and the narrowly scientific approach. It is for educators to restore these qualities of being to their high status.

Keats, in fact, defined the Poetical Character in terms of this energy, this fierce gusto for living:

> As to the Poetical Character itself it is not itself – it is no self – it is everything and nothing – It has no character – it enjoys light and shade: it lives in gusto, be it foul or fair, high or low, rich or poor, mean or elevated – it has as much delight in conceiving an Iago as an Imogen. What shocks the virtuous philosopher, delights the chameleon Poet. It does no harm from its relish of the dark side of things any more than from its taste for the bright one; because they both end in speculation.[33]

By speculation Keats means to imply not theoretical consideration but heightened contemplation, an active state in which all one's faculties are united and infused with what is being created. Whatever the nature of the poet's creation, he finds the experience releasing. He has given shape to his energy. He has extended his understanding of the world. Keats, in one of his letters, talks about

> looking upon the sun, the moon, the stars, the earth and its contents as materials to form greater things – that is to say, ethereal things – but here I am talking like a madman – greater things than our creator himself made.[34]

A madman? Because god-like? Then it is a divine madness and perhaps this is the clue to the Emily Dickinson poem I have already quoted.

The madness consists of seeing through the eye not with it: seeing imaginatively, seeing objects in a state of continual metamorphoses. A discarded engine is nothing to a motor-mechanic's eye but it may be everything to the sculptor.

> For me no object can be tied down to any one sort of reality. A stone may be part of a wall, a piece of sculpture, a lethal weapon, a pebble on a beach or anything else you like, just as this file in my hand can be metamorphosed into a shoe-horn or a spoon, according to the way in which I use it. The first time the importance of this phenomenon struck me was in the trenches during the 1st World War when my batman turned a bucket into a brazier by poking a few holes in it with his bayonet and filling it with coke. For me this commonplace incident had poetic significance; I began to see things in a new way.[35]

Yet in the creation of art our energies can expose us to the most terrifying of experiences. I have already said that great literature often has a highly disturbing content.

This is true and paradoxical for writers not only survive the expressions of their nightmares, they can be uplifted by them.

The greatest tragedies are dense with the sufferings inflicted on man by chance or design, or both. Yet we dip into them again and again for the elation they bring! The reader relives in part the experiences the writers must have felt creating them; the exposure to existence, the attempt to give it circumference and the liberation brought about by so doing. All art is intrinsically affirmative because it is creation.

Literature is valuable because it strives for the completest understanding, the completest fulfilment. Fulfilment first of the writer, then of the reader. Elizabeth Barrett Browning, in a Preface to her Poems sums this up well:

> I have done my work – not as mere hand and head work apart from the personal being but as the completest expression of that being which I could attain.[36]

How similar this is to Sartre's aspiration:

> Metaphysics . . . is the living effort to embrace from within the human condition in its totality.[37]

Poetry *is* the metaphysics of experience.

Four

Why is it that some few individuals feel compelled to contract out of society in its present pursuit of prosperity and success? Why do they feel this need, this desire to break through their immediate circumstances, to transcend the limitations of social class, race, nation? Why is it that one man feels the need for the fundamental and another is content with the superficial? Is it that the latter is brainwashed and the former somehow escapes the surrounding battery of pressures? I believe this is generally the case and wish in this chapter to suggest how it is that some individuals manage to elude the system.

Each poet must have his own unique motivations for writing, complex, half-conscious or unconscious personal motives. Yet, at the same time, one is impressed by how often creation has its source in disturbance, disorder, anxiety. It is as if poets are men highly aware of the chaotic powers that dart beneath the ordered surface of daily life. They are men who have been granted the terrible gift of spiritual sight and who cannot be bought off by any amount of bribery. By the drive of their own nature, almost beyond their own wishes, they are made to search for that which is true, fundamental.

Certainly a reading of Emily Dickinson's work supports these remarks. This is a poem of hers about experience.

> I stepped from plank to plank
> A slow and cautious way;
> The stars about my head I felt,
> About my feet the sea.
>
> I knew not but the next
> Would be my final inch.
> This gave me that precarious gait
> Some call experience.[38]

One can really sense the author's situation. One can imagine the planks, of different lengths, rickety, completely inadequate for the journey. Above her one sees the sky, immense, full of stars, and below, the sea. The great world makes *her* journey look minute, awkward, almost absurd. Yet it is *all* there is, a precarious gait/experience. A precarious gait because she does not know where she is being taken, she must inspect her experience as it unfolds.

Many of Emily Dickinson's poems stem from anxiety, from an inner foreboding, a fear of imminent disaster.

I had a terror since September I could tell to no one and so I sing, as the boy does by the burying ground, because I am afraid.[39]

The paradox expressed here, creation from destruction, singing from terror, is a common one in her poetry. It is crystallized particularly well in her poem 'A Whip'.

> Not with a club the heart is broken,
> Nor with a stone;
> A whip, so small you could not see it—
> I've known
>
> To lash the magic creature
> Till it fell,
> Yet that whip's name too noble
> Then to tell.
>
> Magnanimous of bird
> By boy descried,
> To sing unto the stone
> Of which it died.[40]

The stone is the agent of the bird's death. It is also the cause of the bird's song. Without the suffering there would not be the creation. From the creation comes the energy, the liberation. The suffering is greeted as a necessary enemy and then transcended. In some ways the activity is comparable to psychotherapy; neurosis is created by the suppression of unbearable suffering but as suppression is not extinction, the suffering continues to live at a hidden level, generating conflict, tension, which overwhelms or exhausts the person. Good psychotherapy consists in the person bringing the suffering to the light of consciousness, reliving it, with the consequent freeing of his personality. How similar this is to Emily Dickinson! She has a terror, she experiences it, heightens it even, creates from it and then moves through it.

All this bears out the truth: that to allow experience to happen, to take on the burden of the mystery is the path to greater understanding. In *this* consists the value of art. We are back with the insights of Keats and Melville.

But there is one point. Art is *not* therapy, though it may contain therapeutic elements. Art is not a relieving scream of pain nor a private weeping. Art moves towards circumference, an encompassing, an understanding. Emotion there must be, but also meaning. Work that only expresses feeling is too subjective, too private. Work that only expresses thought is too objective, too public. One needs the fusing of great thought with powerful feeling. The work of art has to go beyond the creator to be relevant for man.

In psychotherapy, the patient stumbling towards a discovery of himself may speak in the most fragmentary and confused of voices – in art the artist stumbling towards a discovery of himself *must* speak in a voice that gives an exact emotional and intellectual equivalence to the movement of his being. If he has the depth of being and the gift with language there may just emerge a new exciting world – a work of art, in which man can delight and ponder over. The artist's quest, like the philosopher's, is the quest of man – or it is nothing.

Five

I hope to have said enough to indicate the nature of the relationship between Literature and life. I have said that literature is the effort to encompass existence in all its complexity or in Emily Dickinson's language, its business is circumference. In this consists its greatest value. But to leave the discussion here would be misleading. Poetry is not just understanding – it is a style of understanding and that style is communicated through the words.

> Great literature is simply language charged with meaning to the utmost possible degree.[41]

Ezra Pound's definition is pertinent. I have talked about the sort of meaning the poet is concerned with, now I must mention his medium, language.

In phrasing it like this, though, I have already implied a division between style and content. I have created a division which cannot, in reality, exist. Style and content are one. The how and the what cannot be separated. A joke told one way is funny, told another way it is dull, told another way, it is sad. In each case the content is identical. It is the method of narration that gives it its meaning. The style interprets the content, in which case, the content depends on the style, the style on the content. They are one. The same idea cannot be expressed in ten different ways: each expression changes the idea, however slightly. This means that we can look at a man's style and, from that, determine the sensitivity of the writer. Crude language embodies a crude thought. Sensitive language embodies a sensitive thought. The greater grasp we have of language the greater grasp we have of our own consciousness. It is only a small step from this position to Ezra Pound's claim:

> If a nation's literature declines, the nation atrophies and decays . . . A people that grows accustomed to sloppy writing is a people in process of losing grip on its empire and itself.[42]

Losing grip is, of course, an understatement of the situation. The mass media have distorted and abused language so much that words connected with love and beauty are almost impossible to use in order to convey what was once their meaning. Consumer trivia have been so poeticized, so sensuously celebrated that the poet has been almost forced into a very small area of experience; the stringent intellectual sphere of Charles Tomlinson or the violent disruptive sphere of Ted Hughes. A fine contemporary poetry of human relationships does not exist. Is it that the mass media by exploiting the language of affection and desire have made such a poetry impossible?

Poetic language, Pound argues, is language charged with the utmost possible meaning. I want to make some of the implications of this definition more explicit. Language has two main functions: to refer and to express. By refer is meant denote – denote an object or a state: that chair, this book, that emotion, this thought. By express is meant the mood which is communicated, how the person feels towards what he is saying. 'This book' could be said derisively or happily. It could be an order 'This book!' or a question 'This book?' The two functions, which can only be analytically separated, have been named denotation and connotation. Language *charged* with meaning would necessarily employ both aspects: if one was absent (in the sense of meaning being obscure or emotion barely felt) it would only be a partial use of language. A slightly pedantic observation in itself yet it has wide-ranging implications. Poetry fully using its medium must, then, bring into dynamic play the two functions of language. The poem must express mood and meaning, emotion and idea, feeling and thought. A poetry that offers only mood, is of its nature limited. A poetry that offers only thought is similarly restricted.

Paul Valéry has defined the real poetry as that having 'a continuous and repeated connection between rhythm and syntax, between sound and sense'.[43] This is exactly it! The poet must be neither seduced by the sounds – though he must love them – nor by the meaning – though the poet is dedicated to it. The writer must be perfectly poised, emotion, thought, imagination, instinct, running together in an act of perfect attention. This alone can create a real poetry.

It is precisely this act which Plato so misunderstood in 'The Republic'. The poet does not indulge his emotions, or encourage others to do so. Art is not only the release of emotion, it is the definition of it. Art involves understanding, as well as expression. Today it is a commonplace that the suppression of emotion is dangerous, yet the very art that refines and directs emotion is despised. The effect of kinetic art, so fashionable, so empty, is merely to confirm the philistine's belief about the uselessness of the arts. He had always said that art was superfluous, unless it was good design that could be exhibited in the house. Kinetic Art is the latest expression in our culture of the merely aesthetic. Can a renaissance take its place? Can we create a full literature again by man for man? If this is at all possible then the way to it must be laid down in our educational system. It is the aim of the next part to show how this might be begun.

PART FIVE

Creativity and the Teaching of English

'We should be looking for people with divergent unorthodox kinds of intelligence, not conformist, orthodox types . . . The aim must be to maximize variation. We need to give all children equal opportunity to learn how to learn but after that they should be encouraged to follow their own special interests instead of the textbook conventions of examination syndicates.'[44]

One

'Creative Writing', the term, has bad connotations – connotations of conscious spontaneity and artificial creativity. Still the term exists and I intend to use it. The aim of this part is to show how creative work can be begun in schools and how it can be directed into maturity.

But what does the term 'creative writing' mean? By it, I mean writing that is primarily expressive of the individual who writes it and is effective in terms of its word energy, its penetration and freshness of perception. It is opposed to 'formal' work: work which aims solely at getting the externals, like punctuation and spelling, right. This isn't to say that creative writing is totally indifferent to these matters. On the contrary, a certain amount of subtlety can be gained through a careful use of punctuation and spelling needs to be fairly accurate to ensure communication. But in itself it is trivial. The impetus of writing should lie beyond externals, in the heart and imagination of the child.

I would like to take just one example here. The following poem was written by a twelve-year-old girl in the bottom stream of a secondary modern school. Technically, the writing is poor, and yet I think the poem shows a real curiosity, the poet's wonder at experience and the poet's precision of detail:

Daddy long legs
The Daddy long legs
cushed along the floor
he has so many legs
I wonder why he is cauld
daddy long legs he is so horrible
so people do not like
daddy long legs. he has a little
body. I wonder where his eyes
are why has he
some many legs sometimes

he comes from no where
and people screamed when they
see him

The lines – 'He has a little body. I wonder where his eyes are. Why has he so many legs. Sometimes he comes from nowhere and people scream' – show an eye for detail and express real experience. Of course the poem as a whole is clumsy, marred by its technical insufficiencies. To widen and deepen this girl's grasp on English would be to increase her power over experience, a power to refine and intensify her feelings and thoughts.

We ought always to remember in the matter of spelling and punctuation, John Clare. Accepted as a fine poet, yet, like some others of his vocation, he could neither spell nor punctuate correctly. It wasn't a source of worry to him. He merely dispensed with punctuation in his later poems! And it is these poems that we admire today.

Creative writing is concerned with the expression of the whole person. Let us not murder it before it exists. Let us not worry over details of formal correctness – nor let us worry about assessing it. If the work is good and embodies the unique, it cannot be marked, it cannot be compared to anything beyond itself. There can be no objectivity. In which case why bother? Why lie?

This section is about creative writing. It is not about the teaching of English but about only one part of it.* English should consist of as much drama and discussion as writing. I do not wish to leave the impression that English teaching *is* creative writing. Nor do I wish to give the impression that creative writing stands by itself. It should be seen as part of the whole: the different areas of activity should interpenetrate and become indivisible. A situation suggested in a poem (literature) can lead to the children acting it out, improvising it (drama) and from that to talking about the morality involved (discussion) to writing about it. Of course there is no intrinsic reason why the theme should stop at the writing. Further exploration might demand all manner of knowledge from other departments. In fact, under the impetus of the experience, subjects break down. This, as I have said, is as it should be. Much more teaching should be done through themes which implicate many areas of knowledge. In this way divisions give way to unity, learning to understanding. Whether this will come about is difficult to say but at least the English teacher can begin it in his own domain, literature, drama, discussion, research, writing, these should all run into each other, parts that form a whole.

To approach the problem of writing I have decided to break my comments into two main parts. Comments on form. Comments on

* In the Teacher's Book to *English Broadsheets* I have commented on the place of drama, discussion and project work in English teaching. The approach to imaginative writing outlined in the following chapters has been more fully developed in the actual Broadsheets.

content. Again these are not to be seen as finally severed from each other. They are divided only to clarify what is rather a complex process.

In the last chapter I wish to describe an actual class taken on the theme of the crucifixion.

Two

'I do believe that a poet should know all he can. No subject is alien to him, and the profounder his knowledge in any direction, the more depth will there be to his poetry. I believe he should be thoroughly grounded in both the old and the new poetic forms, but I am firmly convinced that he must never respect tradition above his intuitive self.' [45]

Amy Lowell's declaration has exactly the right balance. Knowledge is needed, intuition is needed. The poet ought to know the many forms available for his use as this may well extend the range of experience available for his writing. He must know about tradition – and use it where it aids his expression – but, finally, he must be unflinchingly honest to himself. And if tradition or set form prevents this, then it must go! Out! Authenticity rather than hypocrisy, freedom rather than restraint. This position holds true for the poet of integrity and it also holds true for the child as writer. The child needs to explore various forms and styles of writing. He needs to become grounded in the old and new, but, the aim of this is ultimately to release him into his own experience, to which he must be loyal.

How then does this affect our actual teaching? Let us begin with a class that has been taught English in the now largely discredited traditional manner. [46] It happens to be the sort of teaching I have always taken over from so I will use it as my point of departure.

The class has had five periods of English a week, rather like the following:

Monday: Literature. The class reads *The Black Arrow*. It is read in turns round the class. The books are put back in the desks when the bell goes.

Tuesday: Grammar. The class divides simple sentences into their component parts. Ten sentences have been given. Towards the end of the lesson they correct their work and a mark out of ten is given.

Wednesday: Creative work. Two titles are put on the board, 'A visit to my Grandfather', 'A day at the zoo'. The composition is to be two or three sides and the mark will be added to others at the end of the term to arrive at their English percentages.

Thursday: Verse. An animal poem is read out. The class has to write a piece of verse describing one of the animals at the zoo. Rhymes are not expected. An 'experimental' lesson.

Friday: Comprehension. Page 30 – read the passage and then answer questions a to e. The work is to be done silently. Marks will be allotted.

I do not think it is necessary for me to comment at length on these standard lessons. It must be clear to the reader by now how such teaching kills the living child, institutes the mechanical robot. In these examples it is done by a combination of forces, the marking and competitive system, the content of the lesson, and the form of work asked for. I wish to confine my comments to the two creative lessons.

The composition lesson: the subject matter concerns conventional events, the Sunday trip to the grandparents, the holiday visit to the zoo. Conventional events require conventional treatment . . . unless of course the teacher can break through the surface of the experience. What for instance is Grandfather like if he is woken up from his afternoon sleep? What does he say? And Grandmother? What does she do? Look like? But there has been no discussion before the titles have been put up. The teacher wants to hold by the convention as convention – and he wants two sides of it. This requirement reinforces the notion that the teacher wants to exclude reality. The experience may be adequately conveyed for the child in half a page – but two pages have been demanded! The problem is to fill the two sides. That must be concentrated on. Forget the experience. Keep to the convention. Besides, the work is going to be marked. One must play safe.

What has been achieved in this lesson? The complete severing of writing from experience: writing is something you do in school; life is outside, something different. Is it any wonder our society believes that literature is a waste of time?

The 'experimental' lesson calls for less comment. It is dead in the same way as the composition lesson. The children have to write about animals. What animals? In what situations? It is left vague. The lesson is 'experimental' because the children don't have to use rhymes. A euphemism of course. The children know the teacher really believes that poetry has to rhyme. The lesson – worse than a waste of time because of the pernicious assumptions it conveys to the children.

What are we to do with such a form? We must present some specific and powerful situations which shock the children into experience, and we must present a variety of new forms in which they will be able to express themselves. In a sense these two must run into each other. The last thing to be created is a division between exercises and applications. The child must always write about what is real and immediate to his

E

imagination, but sometimes he will be working with a particular form in mind, at others he will be completely free to write as he wishes. The balance is delicate and depends totally on the teacher. The spirit is everything. The law nothing.

In this chapter I wish to talk about forms. In the next, content. The division is merely one of convenience, to help clarify what is a complex, and ideally, indivisible process.

Up to now the child's experience of writing has been one of restriction. He has been held in, cramped. Let him sense the freedom of writing. Let him write about what he wants, how he wants. To do that, exercise books must go. Sheets of paper are much better. Let him write spontaneously. Let him keep it, or throw it away or show it to the class as he wishes. There should be no standards to begin with. No marking. No censorship. If the child is pleased with his work he will write it up carefully and want to keep it. A folder should be provided for this purpose.

Perhaps a good way of beginning is with some music. The children have the loose paper on their desk. They can listen to Stravinsky's 'The Rite of Spring' (opening movement) or to Mahler's Storm movement (symphony no 1, opening of 4th movement).

As the children listen they are to scrawl down all the pictures, thoughts, feelings that run through their minds. Then as the music is played for the second time, they are asked to work on their jottings, to write it up in any sequence they want.

Here is a piece of work by a fourth-year fifth-stream boy, written in this manner to Stravinsky:

Steam

Waiting. Suddenly the light flashes from red to green. The wheels gradually turn and a joint is hit and the sound echoes off the rounded walls. The noises increases as we gain speed. A round circle of light appears. We make our way towards it. It grows and soon we rush from darkness into light. Then a steady rocking motion begins. From side to side, side to side, and side to side. Up and down and up and down.

In the distance a plume of smoke appears. Coming nearer we hear the roar of the metal monster. Its huge exhaust beats, shattering the quiet countryside. The metal monster sings its songs to the high hills. Gradually the countryside is covered in its dark exhaust. The ground beneath us vibrates as its climbs with its load the last few yards to the summit. Then its exhaust beat stops. The train curves gracefully over the summit with the brake disappearing with its bright red lamp. It coasts on. Gaining speed. Rushing through cuttings and tunnels, stations and villages, over bridges. Racing cars and aeroplanes. Passing lonely houses and deserted moorland roads. Then gradually the brakes are applied and it is brought to a noisy standstill in the big city.

It is quite possible that not every child will have gained from this opening lesson. Some children, after lessons with so much content given, will feel rather lost. But it is a beginning – and no judgements are made by the teacher.

Free writing from music can easily move into free verse. When jotting his ideas down to the music, the child most probably will have listed them like this:

> drums beating faster
> a lion running
> herds of gazelles
> thunder

This technique of breaking the line at the end of an idea and starting another on the next is one employed by free verse. In free verse the line, as opposed to the metre, creates the unit. Each line is a movement, a thought or a feeling, a quality or an action. Many Whitman, Lawrence and Hughes poems could be used here. It is important though that the child is not presented with the technique conceptually, in the abstract. After reading and discussing, say Lawrence's *Mountain Lion*, the children could be asked to return to the poem and see how each line marks a movement:

> Men!
> Two men!
> Man! The only animal in the world to fear!
> They hesitate.
> We hesitate.
> They have a gun.
> We have no gun.

Seeing the technique is understanding it and understanding it is being able to use it. Free verse should only be asked for, however, when the stimulus for writing is intense, and demands a poetic energy. Here is a poem by a first-year boy – following such a lesson.

Whale at Sea

The harpoon was ready.
Whale ahoy! cried the first mate.
The bitter arctic wind blew across the deck.
It nipped through my thick furs.
Harpoon on target —
FIRE!
Thud went the harpoon into the whale's thick blubber.
The sensation of satisfaction tingled through my body as I hit it.
The water was red and disturbed.
It was giving us quite a struggle.
It wasn't dead yet.
A feeling of tenseness, wondering whether to put another harpoon in it.
But it was all over.
The whale was dead.

The children quickly assimilate the idea of free form and tend to prefer it to more formal writing. The move from 'free verse' into imagism is straightforward. In imagism, the image forms the line. The power of the poem comes to rest on the vivid and unexpected comparison of one thing to another. T. E. Hulme's poem is by now a classic imagist poem:

> A touch of cold in the autumn night —
> I walked abroad
> And saw the ruddy moon lean over a hedge
> Like a red-faced farmer.
> I did not stop to speak, but nodded,
> And round about were the wistful stars
> With white faces like town children.

Images can involve a great deal of originality and fun and children find it a most accessible form:

> He comes in flying about
> Hitting the walls like a blind bat.
> His beak like a blackberry thorn,
> His wings when open look like leaves.
> His feet are like a piece of string tied together
> In knots, black as soot.
>
>   (by a first-year girl)

Life

Shower of sparks fall
One by one they go out – dead.
One catches, remains, grows,
A small flame, growing, growing
Getting brighter, jumping higher,
Consuming, scorching everything near.
Slowly falling, fading, dying
Lower and lower.
One bright spark – then gone.
Blackness – nothing.

(by a Sixth-form boy)

Dust

Man was from dust
He will return to dust.
His mushroom-clouds will burn him
as a dust-mote in a furnace.
His friendly atoms will shred him
And his children will go with him.
His flesh will drop and crumble,
his bones will totter and fall.
His cities will fall, his towns will vanish,
his work will be lost, his soul will be vanquished —
Man is dust
and he will reach the sea.

(Fifth-form boy)

Children have a very vivid style of apprehending the world. Our job is to bring it alive in the class-room and extend it. Again and again one is startled by the fusion of the expected with the unexpected – 'the lightning leapt like a frog', 'Crow – the devil's pandar, thief of nature', 'Death is like coming to the top of the stairs.'

Images can become bizarre and extravagant. This, at a later stage, will have to be checked. But for the moment the child should be enjoying the powers of his own originality. He should be enjoying writing – *his* writing. We have already come a long way.

Again, shape-poems are enjoyable to create. Here there are any number of good examples which can be used: Herbert, Dylan Thomas, Apollinaire, Lewis Carroll. Here is a poem by a first-year boy:

My   Cat
is stupid and
looks putrid
it says
that
its
a boxer
like Clay
But I don't
think so because
all she does
is play And
She has a long *long windy* *strands* *furry tail*

From shape we can quickly move to writing that uses its typography. If the line is telling you where to pause and for how long, punctuation and capitals can be dispensed with. The poem is given a typographical purity. This has been used a lot in modern poetry: in William Carlos Williams, Charles Tomlinson, e. e. cummings, Roger McGough. Here is a poem by a fifth-year boy after looking at McGough's *Dreampoem*:

There was a Time

There was a time when I
                small boy
                       would jump and run
through towering grass and groping trees
    triumphant in my speed and nerve.

When we
        polluted water paddling
                        caught fish half drugged
        drowning them in jars.
When we
    stackwreckers
                would race a red bellowing farmer home
            never to be caught.
When we
    impossiblewallscaling
                            would jump stiff limbed
        to sicken on green fruit.
When we
    hiding place sitting
        one drag passing
            would crouch laughing choking
with unbelieved taletelling that puzzled all.
Then as unseen education tightened its grip
    and parents turned to the future
we were shoved and pushed unknowing
                        in tight moulds
    stifling us for a world
        uniformity wanting
                    frowning at
simple childish joys.
        Now is the time when you
                    child watching
                    play watching
    feel a twinge of
        good years gone.

The tyranny of the conventional, the two-page composition or the rhyming poem should by now be broken. A new means of expression, more powerful, more flexible, allowing for greater honesty, has been opened up. A term or two terms may have passed – it must be remembered that this work is not done in isolation. Developing from it and alongside it there has been discussion, drama, research. The techniques are not presented one on top of the other. Between each there has been plenty of writing with form unspecified. The rate of the movement cannot be stated because it should depend entirely on the needs of the children as the teacher interprets them.

But now we can return to more formal patterns of expression. The children have had freedom, now they can try discipline.

Popular songs, today and in primitive societies, have always made good use of repetition to heighten emotion. It can be seen at work also in political speeches and advertising – in prayer and in children's taunts. Here is a poem by a fourth-year girl using repetition to persuade the reader of her views:

Death of the Hippies

The publicity man has killed them all,
Leaving remains of love, happiness, no war,
Rusty bells form ugly graves,
For all the once beautiful people,
Autumn comes, the flowers are drooping,
Death, death to the love generation.

The publicity man has killed them all,
By giving two-year-olds bells to wear.
They don't know it, but parents do,
Their parents know the damage caused.
Here them cry as they laugh together,
'Death, death to the love generation!'

The publicity man has killed them all
But their revenge will soon come to him.
An end to the hippies, their flowers and bells,
But they soon will be replaced,
And hippies themselves will then be crying,
'Death, death to the love generation!'

And here is another poem by a fourth-year girl which effectively uses repetition to create tension:

Distant Drumming

A faint drumming was all that could be heard, in the still warm air. The faraway sound – a distant drumming.
How far away no one could tell, but there was always that sound – a distant drumming.
A wave of scarlet came over the hill, a distant hill, and still – a distant drumming.
A flash of steel along the wave of red: weapons to kill – a distant drumming.
Fear and hate in the waiting hearts, an urge to break the sound of – a distant drumming.
How long now? Have they reached the valley? The beat no longer comes from – a distant drumming.
The people glanced around them – at their homes in the valley. The valley which echoed with – a distant drumming.

The wave of scarlet rose and destroyed. The wounded lay dying – a distant
    drumming.
Over the hill, the only noise: the faint retreating sound – a distant
    drumming.

From repetition we can move to popular song in which rhyme and
rhythm also play an important part. The following street songs were
written for a market scene in a free-drama lesson:

> Pork Pies! Pork Pies! I sell pork pies!
> Big pies, Small pies. I sell wide pies.
> I sell pies that Pop your eyes.
>
> Pies! Pies! Lovely hot pies!
> Come taste —
> Make haste!
> Fresh meat
> WHAT A TREAT!
> Pies! Pies! Lovely hot pies!
>
> Selling Fish! Selling Fish!
> They're twice as big
> As the biggest dish!
> I am behind this stall
> All day long
> Won't you come and buy some fish.
> So I can stop singing my song.
>
> Fish and chips! Fish and chips!
> Come and buy my fish and chips.
> Nice, and hot
> That's what I've got.
> Smashing gorgeous fish and chips!
>
> Some pies are cold.
> Some pies are hot.
> I like the pies that *you haven't got.*
>
> Who wants fish from your stall
> For they're thin and small.
> They taste like they'd been done for three days
> So you might as well throw them away.
>
> Fish and chips! Fish and chips!
> Why should I buy your fish and chips!
> Nice and hot?
> Cold the lot!
> That's all you've got.

Having arrived at the use of rhyme we can move into nonsense poems which exploit rhyme to maximum advantage and then into ballads. Here is a ballad by a fourth-year girl which shows great mastery over the power of rhyme.

The Burn-up

We sprang to our Nortons,
Dick, Paddy and me.
I revved up, Dick revved up,
We revved up all three.

'Stop!' cried the copper
As we all pelted by.
'Stop us?' yelled Paddy —
'You wanna try!'

Straight past the café
And on through the town.
Funny how each copper
Tried flagging us down.

I watched my speedo move
From seventy and up ten.
Three Nortons dicing it
With three speed-mad men.

Nearing the crossroads
I changed down to third,
Dick opened his throttle —
Flew past like a bird.

But danger was close now,
Dick never knew
Three men on three Nortons
Would soon become two.

Hit the lorry at ninety —
Killed outright.
Dick and his Norton
Found heaven that night.

I hope to have written and quoted enough to illustrate how some of the major forms of poetry can be introduced to the child. I have written more about the freer forms because these are the ones that tend to be ignored. In fact most conventional teaching had made some sort of room for formal poetry. It was the way that it was done that was at fault.

Ultimately one aims at a class-room situation where one can always say 'Choose the form you want to write in'. To achieve this the child must be aware of the available choices. It has been the aim of this chapter to show how this can be done. I want now to consider the subject matter of the English lesson. What type of situations should children be asked to write about?

Three

What should children be asked to write about? Anything, providing it can stimulate their imaginations, move their feelings, arouse their curiosities. The teacher can bring a situation *to* the children through any number of ways – passages from novels, excerpts from newspapers, poems, plays, photographs, reproductions, music and song. Or he can let the children present, in discussion, *their* situations, their conflicts, memories, dreams, fantasies, anxieties and beliefs. Indeed if the right relationship with a class can be formed there becomes *too* much to do, too much to talk about, too much to write about. The bell becomes an obtrusive enemy, breaking up the enjoyment of discovery.

Broadly speaking the first method, the teacher presenting the situation, is out to encourage the child to extend his understanding of the world through imaginative projection. The child may be asked to release an animal from a trap. He may be asked to march in a revolution. He may be asked to be Icarus soaring towards the sun, or to be an old man looking out of the window on life. The child has here to work from his limited experience to depart into something else, something greater and unknown.

The second method is out to encourage, not an outward flight of the imagination, but an inward search. The child may have to recall a squabble with his friend, why it happened, what his feelings were, what results it had, and then be asked to reconstruct it in his writing. He may have to recall a bad dream, or a very early memory or an absurd prank and so on. In this sort of writing a complete honesty to the experience is required. But, of course, the child must, at the same time, feel free to imagine the situation if he prefers to. The two methods are *not* rigid divisions. Rigid divisions cannot possibly exist in such work. It is merely a matter of emphasis: the first is more concerned with something outside the child, the second more concerned with what is within.

Yet the writing and exploration we are out to promote cannot exist at once, for it will depend on a trusting relationship between the children and the teacher. This is more easy to establish with eleven-year-olds than with teenagers who are more suspicious, more self-conscious, more worried about the disturbing aspects of life. In either case a good relationship cannot exist over-night but if it doesn't come to exist the work cannot be done in any real or satisfying way.

At the beginning of the work I have argued the teacher must accept what the children write. There should be no marking, no assessing, no comments in red ink like 'scruffy', 'do it again', 'see me'. This is essential if the teacher is to create an atmosphere in which imagination thrives. In the classroom there should be a sense of freedom, of enjoyment and spontaneity. Nevertheless the teacher has to move carefully. He cannot suddenly enter the children's world. Teacher and pupils are strangers at first, both curious about the other, both a little frightened, both waiting.

It is helpful, I think, to begin outside the direct experience of the children. I have already suggested that Mahler's 'Storm Movement' or Stravinsky's 'Rite of Spring' (or, equally as exciting, the third of Britten's 'Four Sea Interludes') is an effective way of beginning to stimulate good writing. Now the music invariably suggests movements in nature. The Stravinsky conjures up a primitive world, a world of wild animals – at once beautiful and ferocious. The Mahler conjures up turbulence and upheaval, earthquakes, sea storms, blizzards, at once elating and dangerous. The children find the music exciting and also the themes it suggests to them are outside their immediate realm of experience. They have no need to fear what they write down.

From here one can move forward to a consideration of animals. Many of the nature poems of D. H. Lawrence and Ted Hughes are particularly useful for they concentrate on the otherness of animals and at the same time employ a free verse form (which in the last chapter I suggested was a good way of developing from free writing). The step from animals to man is an easy one. A class cannot talk long about animals before the problems of man's interference with nature enters the discussion. Whether one takes industry, trade, sport, the history of man's attitudes to animals is a questionable one and continues to be so. In the discussion of these issues the teacher has moved into man – into man's way of treating animals. Now when the teacher feels ready he can leap from this relation into that between man and man.

It is perhaps best to begin with the children's own experience, their games, their friends, their fights, their pranks. And from here? Anywhere! Into the family, the school, the wider society, or inwards, into the child's own apprehension of Life and Death.

I feel there is no better way of illustrating what I mean than by showing a selection of children's writing. I have divided the work into the various themes suggested in this chapter.

1. Nature
2. Childhood
3. Family

4. Society
5. Death
6. Religion

I have decided not to comment on the pieces partly because I think the writing speaks very well for itself and, also, because I would like the reader to make up his own mind about the value and implications of such work.

Nature

1. The Fox

The bright eyes stared back
Frightened, waiting for me
To finish
To close them for ever.
Yesterday I would have laughed
At the thought of feeling sorry
For a trapped animal
But not now.
Its body shivered – one bad leg
Lying still, immobile.
A yard away lay a dead bird
Caught by the fox before?
Survival is the law of nature
But not the law of man.
As I neared those ugly steel jaws
The animal flinched
Tried to pull away
But could not.
Suddenly its own jaw opened
Showing rows of strong, sharp teeth
And for one moment I lost my pity —
But then it shrank back
That immobile leg
Tearing at the joint.
Pain.
The fox
A hated, hunted animal
And suddenly I could not watch it any longer.
I pointed the gun at it
And . . .
The body lay still
I felt like Hitler should have felt
But there was no more pain
No more hunting
No more fight for survival
Man had won.   (Sixth-form girl)

69

2. Death of an Animal

Stalking, creeping, animal-seeking,
The hunter descends on his prey,
Eyes reflecting, sparkling, neon lights,
Bloodthirsty in their own uncommon way.

A fateful spring! The gun goes off,
With a shattering roar, stabbing light streaks out,
The sound's intense and above it all,
Is the final squealing death-bound call.

A hare no more, just a bloody mess,
Its nerves twitching in its final death roll,
Blood oozing from vicious wounds,
A dead mass without a soul.

(Second-year boy)

3. The Spider

Yesterday bright sun lit up the blackberry hedge.
The green paradise for birds and insects.
Today the mist leaves drops of moisture wherever they will cling.
That same hedge that yesterday was so green and fresh
Is shaded by a film of water drops
Suspended half an inch above the leaves and fruit.
Delicate patterns come alive, the spider has its death-trap here,
Which unsuspecting tiny fly would yesterday have settled
But today will see the danger
And keep away, hovering above its death.
There is no resting place for the weary insect
Until it falls to its death,
To be devoured at the spider's leisure.

(Fourth-year girl)

4. King Fisher!

The fish swam through the cool clear water,
The kingfisher fledglings squawked.
They were hungry.
The bird returned
And, seeing the hungry fledglings with gaping beaks,
Hopped out on to a branch sticking out of the bank,
She saw the fish, and with a sudden flash of blue and gold, dived.
Only a second was needed to stab the writhing fish,
With one gulp she swallowed it, head first, and dived after
   another, to feed her fledglings.

(First-year boy)

5. The Seahorse

Your domain is the green murky waters
Which slothfully lick and curl round lichen rocks and
Obscure crevises – harbouring evil.
This is the den of the pirhana and grimacing shark
Whose ravenous, glaring eyes glint in artful harmony
With pointed teeth, while lurking for prey.
Yet this same world can be transformed to fantasy.
From within time-worn caverns, by corals, anemones and fern
   you emerge;
Your slender, sculptured body, erect in its coat
Of scaly mail and spicular spine.
Your comical tubular snout and prehensile tail
Make you a creature of charm, rather than purpose.
Your eye does not sneer or glare, but is glazed,
Sensitive to infinite time and apparent thought.
But time has no meaning here – you were not born,
You do not die – you were created a million years ago
And time has not altered you or penetrated your domain.
You just exist in your world of blurred silence and preferred
   solitude.

(Sixth-form girl)

6. The Storm

The sky is as black as night. The rain is pouring down, as though the sky has been emptied out. The wind has turned the sea into mountainous waves and our boat is tossed about like a cork. The lightning flashes and lightens the whole sky as though a searchlight had been switched on. The thunder is so great that the whole earth seems to tremble. We in our tiny boat feel just like a match-stick floating in the middle of the ocean. Although we had intended to spend many hours cruising round the bay we now are fighting our way back home against the head-on wind, and it seems as though we are going backwards instead of forwards.

(First-year girl)

Childhood

1

Monday Morning came I got up, got dressed and went downstairs for my breakfast, there on the table was a bowl of porridge, 'Ugh, porridge', I said 'I hate porridge'. 'now come on, sit down and eat it, it will do you good,' said Mum looking annoyed. 'No!, I don't want it', 'fair enough' said mum, 'I'll throw it away'. 'You do that' I said angrily, that morning I went off to school in a mood, when I got to school I stood against the radiators talking to my freind when Rosalind Ponce came up, she was a little Bossy boots, a prefect, 'Out' she said in a rude manner. 'No'. I said 'NO' said my freind, 'Did you hear me, I said get out! now go on get out!' 'If you say please we might consider it' I said, 'Now look here' said Bossy Boots 'Who wants to look at you' I said laughing I'm a prefect' said Bossy Boots, 'Oh goody for you' said Susanne (my freind) 'Listen' said Bossy Boots 'Listen! Lady Mucks talking' said Sue. Bossy boots went red in the face and said, 'Right, I want a four page essay from you my girl' 'You'll be lucky if you get anything from us' said sue, 'Yea' I said, Teresa Perkins another freind started mucking about, She smiled at Bossy boots and said, 'come here a minute', Bossy Boots walked over, then teresa said, ''ere Bossy your not funny you Just smell strong, ha, ha, ha.' That did it. Bossy said 'and I want a ten page essay from you too,' she marched off purple in the face.

(Second-year girl)

Me,
     Tich, Mike an' Phil
    Had a game of footer
      An' knocked it through ole man Tucker's window
   So we went in to get it out.
   'No!' he yelled. 'Get lost!'
                     So we mooched around the back
of 'is garage an' lobbed stones at 'im.
               Then
  'E came out chasin' us so
    We ran round the garages to our den
              We lobbed stones at 'im
and 'e yelled unrepeatable words
Ya, ya, ya yelled Phil back at him
    Then, someone's 'ead stuck out of
ole man Tucker's window
         so
we started wavin' at 'im an' 'e
started wavin' 'is fist at us
         so
          we
    went to 'is garden
              me
                 an' Phil
     an'
       knocked a few
     spuds while
              Tich an' Mike made
     a fire
        The spuds were
     great
             but
Ole man Tucker told our Mum
     'an she
   'ALF MURDERED ME!

                            (First-year boy)

3. Memories

The cellar
      so dim and
foreboding
Hazy shadows
cast by candle stubs
           take shape
on the coal dust.
The air
     damp and stagnant
hangs
about my head.
    All is quiet
except
for the footfalls
          on the stone staircase.
The thrill
of blowing out the candles
          while seated on
father's shoulder.
Childhood memories
         trivial
  but treasured
if only the truth were known.

                    (Fifth-year boy)

4. The Visitor

It was the beginning of a new day. A thin white sun rose over the bleak hills; black silhouettes of trees looked brittle against the pale skies. The ground was hard and dry, and around a small, whitewashed cottage the frosted grass seemed to be bristling, as if anticipating the approach of an intruder. This cottage was the only sign of civilization for miles around.

Inside the cottage, McGill was lying on an old coat he had found the previous day. He lay there a long time, staring up at the thatch sticking through the beams of the roof, and thinking. A narrow shaft of sunlight caught his eye. It was coming through a hole in the door. It seemed as if its very brightness had pierced through the door. It made a little spot of light appear on the smooth, earthen floor. It flickered, as if winking at him. McGill watched it for a while, and then it occurred to him that someone might be outside. He got up and pushed his long, black hair out of his eyes, and went to the door. He paused, fingering his rough, black beard, and then lifted the latch. The door swung open.

Outside stood a child, about eight or perhaps twelve years old: it was hard to say. Her large green eyes gazed up at him. 'May I come in?' she said. She almost whispered it. McGill thought for a moment, and then drew back to let her in.

She stepped lightly inside, and sat down on a little wooden stool by the fire. McGill stared at her. Her frame was so small and frail, and he was almost afraid that she would melt before the fire. He could see her more clearly now, for the fire lit up her quaint features. She had red, wispy hair, and a pale skin, which looked as cold as marble. She wore a light cotton dress, and on her feet no shoes, so that her toes twitched with the warmth of the fire, which was very meagre, and McGill felt ashamed.

McGill asked her if she would like something warm to drink. She answered, yes, a little milk. He gave it to her in a wooden bowl, and when she took it, her tiny hands curled round it like tendrils round a smooth tree-trunk. She sipped at it, and said that it was good. This pleased McGill, and he smiled secretly to himself.

When she had finished, she stood up and said that she had to go. McGill did not argue, but unlatched the door and pulled it open for her. On the doorstep she paused and looked up at him. She reached up, and curled her tiny hands around his neck, and kissed his rough hairy cheek with ice-cold lips. Then she was gone.

Every day she came, and every day she sat by the fire and drank a

78

little milk with McGill. And he grew to love her, and called her his fairy-child, and when she left, he only lived to see her come again.

But one day she did not come. And many times that day McGill opened his door and called for her, but still she did not come. The next day she also did not visit him, and McGill spent his time searching for her in the hills, but there was no sign of her.

After three days, McGill decided to go down into the village in the valley and look for her.

When he arrived there, he was laughed at and scorned, and he could not breathe, for the air was choked with mocking voices and cruel thoughts. But he had to find her.

Then he saw her. She was holding the hand of a burly, well-dressed woman who was scolding her for something. The child was crying. McGill saw that she had shoes on her feet, and her hair was combed and tied back with a green ribbon. She turned and caught sight of him – her eyes were unchanged. She held out her slender white arms to him, and McGill ran to gather her into his arms. The woman screamed something incomprehensible to McGill, and tried to pull her away from him. McGill was angry for the first time in his life. He did not like the feeling; but all he knew was that he wanted to stop this woman screaming and pulling the child away from him. He wanted to get up into the clean, pure air of the hills, and take the child with him. He closed his hands around the woman's neck, and in a few minutes she lay quietly on the cobbled road, motionless. McGill turned to pick up the child, but in a moment iron arms seized him, and he was dragged away, frustrated and bewildered.

(Fifth-year girl)

A small child ran
through the foam of the sea of time
laughing at the clouds of despair
which adults in their wisdom
took too seriously —
The sand under her feet was soft —
The only stones were those on which her parents stood.
Where is she now?
She's here
under the cloud,
taking the stones from her shoes.

(Fifth-year girl)

Family

1. In Trouble

In her room the child lay in her bed, gazing round at the weird, frightening shapes over her head. Those shapes, how horrible they looked! The curtains drew in and out as they were sucked up by the breeze of the open window. The shapes appeared to move freely now as if they were coming straight at her.

She crawled under the bed-clothes, shaking, sweat pouring off her as she lay in the heat of her bed. She longed to call out to her mother, but no sound came; she was thinking of the previous night's happenings – the trouble.

Suddenly a cat outside miaowed. Crash! A dustbin lid clattered to the ground. The child lay cowering in her bed. Her hair was sticking to her hot, clammy skin, and she was having difficulty breathing under the bed-clothes. How she longed to get out of the mass of hot sheets and blankets to lay her head on her pillow and breathe normally again! But she shuddered as she remembered – the bad man was waiting for her! Every night, he came, standing over her, frightening her. 'Oh, Mum!' How she longed to call out, but no, she'd only get a slap!

Once again, the curtains were drawn in and out, the heat in her bed, became unbearable. She struggled to lift her head above the bed-clothes.

'Mum!'

A shout in the darkness of the night, in a still, quiet house. The child waited for the lovely sound of her mother's voice.

'Oh Mum, please, Mum!'

Still no sound – but listen, there's a sound.

'Yes, what do you want?'

The sleepy sound came from her parents' room next door.

The child did not answer. She lay there, thankful for her mother's voice. But what if she slaps me again? Fear flooded back over her.

The door squeaked open and her mother entered, yawning.

'Well?' she asked. 'What is it tonight?'

The child brought her head out into the coolness of her room. She stared at the floor and suddenly turned her head to the pillow, as her mother switched on a small bedside lamp. Slowly, wincing, the child turned to face her mother, whose face was tired and drawn.

'N-n-n-nothing, Mum,' she answered in a small voice.

Quickly cold air rushed into her bed and the tears flowed as the smack that followed smarted.

'Oh Mum, Mum, I'm sorry, I didn't mean to wake you. I'm sorry, honest, Mum, honest!' The words gabbled and rushed out of her mouth.

'Sorry?' her mother retorted. 'You don't know the meaning of the word!' Slap! Another slap stung her legs.

The child's screams filled the house and all of a sudden her father came rushing into the room.

'Jo, whatever's . . .?' He stops as he sees his wife sink on to the bed upset. The child lies sobbing in her cold bed. She shivers.

'Oh Daddy, Daddy, I'm sorry. Please believe me, please!'

'Oh Linda, we've told you not to wake us up every night. Look at the time, 3.15. Why do you do it? Why do you wake your mother up every night?'

'I – I don't know, Daddy, I don't know!' Linda pleads. A voice in the back of her mind tells her. 'Go on, tell him the truth, tell him.' But still just the words, 'I don't know' come out of her mouth.

'Very well, Linda, if you don't know why, you can't tell us!' Her father leads his wife by the elbow out of the room, switching off the lamp as they go.

Silence. Hot tears well up in the child's eyes. 'Oh Mum, please come back, I'm sorry, Mum, honest!' Linda pleads in her mind as she dives under the clothes once again, cowering under the bed-clothes as the shapes around her dance on the walls and ceiling.

The poor frightened child sobs as she lies there, shaking, afraid of the creature of her imagination, 'the bad man' . . .

Slowly, she cries herself to sleep.

(Third-year girl)

2. Experiences*

Clare entered the room. 'Mum,' she said, 'Where's my book *Kissing is for Lovers*'?

'Clare, why don't you stop reading romantic books? Go out with some boys. Get yourself a steady boyfriend. You're twenty and you haven't been out with a boy for more than six months. Do something wrong for God's sake. You're too angelic. At times I don't know whether you're human or not, I don't even get to meet any of your girl friends either. You never have brought anyone home have you?'

'Mum,' replied Clare despondently, 'How can I bring my friends home with you flaunting sex and your love of it over the place. You're not ashamed of anything. You don't care who knows about me being illegitimate. If anybody came here, besides relations, they would go home disgusted. I know you are cheap. Don't expect me to be like it. I won't. I'm proud of my virginity.'

'Clare Twomey that's not fair, talking to your own mother like that!' her mother screamed.

Clare's father stood outside listening to the row. Within him raged a battle whether to walk in and make a preference or to leave it and get confronted later. He moved away after hearing the shouting die down. As he did so Clare came tearing out of the room towards her bedroom. In her bedroom she flung herself on her bed and started to cry.

Quarter of an hour later when her crying had subsided she began to think of incidents in her life which had made her so afraid of sex.

Her thoughts went back to that awful day when she was five and didn't understand. She was playing near the haystack on their farm. As she went nearer she heard laughter, a boy and a girl's laughter. She moved nearer as she wanted to romp in the hay. She heard a girl's moan. Then she rounded the haystack. She saw Mary, a girl from the village, and Pete, a farmhand in the hay. She turned and ran. As she ran Peter threatened to kill her if she told anyone.

She ran into her own little den or hideout she had made in the hedge and cried.

* I include this passage in the anthology because it raises many interesting problems. To what extent has the writing been influenced by pulp literature? To what extent does it show an attempt to describe sincerely felt difficulties concerning sex? Is such a preoccupation with sex unhealthy at the age of thirteen? What form of comment should the teacher make at the foot of the story? Should he read the story back to the class and discuss the content openly or should he return it privately to the pupil?
What would the reader have done?

When she finally arrived home, she was very late for tea. Her mother asked why she had been crying. Clare reluctantly explained why.

As Clare thought back, she wondered if it might have been better if her mother had told her that they were doing wrong. Instead all she said was that they were having fun. She also added that she, Clare, would have the same type of fun when she was older but she must be careful of pregnancy. Pregnancy, she remembered how she had pondered over that word pregnancy. She could not think what it meant so she gave up in the end. She daren't ask her mother, for her mother would say that she'd understand later, but that was no good, she had wanted to understand then.

She was thinking of a time five years later when her father entered her bedroom. He looked worried.

'What was the row about this time?' he asked.

'Oh Dad, it was the same topic – why don't I have a boy-friend.'

'Well why don't you?' he retorted angrily.

'I've told you before, Dad. Do I have to tell you again?' she cried at him.

'No I s'pose you don't,' he answered thoughtfully. He left her on the brink of tears again. After he closed the door, she thought back to the time when a man had attempted to sexually assault her. She had been ten at the time.

She was walking home from Ballet classes. She was just by Pete Smith's house when a man came from behind and clasped a hand over her mouth. He pulled at her dress and ripped it. She shivered – she could remember it as if it was yesterday. She remembered how he began to undress and tried to pull her into the field next door, still keeping a hand over her mouth. Ugh! She shivered again when she thought of how hard she kicked him. He was doubled up in agony. She screamed, it was a shriek of a scream, a high piercing shriek.

It seemed like hours later when Fred Smith came running out. He grabbed the man. She was free.

Later the court awarded her compensation – but the damage was done. She would be afraid of sex for the rest of her life. A policewoman gave her a lecture on how to look after herself if she got in that position again.

There was another let down when she started to go out with boys. The first boy she went out with was a drip. Then every boy since then, all they wanted was sex. She cowered away from the thought.

Once she thought that some were different. There was one boy who

84

didn't ask anything from her. She had been going out with him for six months when one day he took her to an upstairs room in a club in London. He betrayed her trust. He tried to remove her virginity. She used the tactics the policewoman taught her. She dived out of the door. Once outside the room she ran and ran until she bumped into a woman. Clare didn't have enough money to get home. This woman and she got talking. That was stupid, thought Clare now. The woman suggested that Clare stayed the night at her flat. Clare agreed as she could do nothing else really.

She went with the woman (whose name was Lily) to her flat. Clare sat down and the woman cooked supper. Then she smoothed away Clare's headache, she looked after her as if she were her lover.

Later Lily lent Clare her nightdress. Lily secretly admired Clare's beauty. Then Lily told Clare she could use her bed. Clare was tucked in by Lily.

The next morning Lily woke Clare up and cooked breakfast. About nine o'clock in the morning another woman entered the flat. When she saw Clare she flew at her in a raging temper.

'Get out of here, you thief, Lily's mine, don't you come in here breaking us up!' Her exact words, thought Clare.

It didn't take Clare long to realize she was involved with Lesbians. She quickly removed herself.

Afterwards she explained to her mother about her experience. All her mother said was that it served her right. She should have stayed in the Club room with Mike.

After the memories had settled again Clare had calmed down slightly, but not for long. She was watching TV. She was soon annoyed again because there was a sexy play on. It was all about adultery and infidelity and divorce, a sex-ridden thing. Then about ten o'clock her mother gave a forced yawn. Here goes, thought Clare. Then true to life, her mother said, 'Ooh I'm tired. I think I'll go to bed. Good night. Don't be late will you, luv.' As usual there was the normal twinkle in her eye and the coaxing of her voice.

Clare knew what her father and mother would do. It was mother's kind of fun. Then to form, about ten minutes later, her father forced a yawn too. He said, 'Good night.'

Five minutes later Clare heard her Mother's precarious giggles. Clare didn't know why her mother and father acted the way they did. Clare began to feel frustrated, left out, lonely. She knew then she must leave. She would go to her Aunt Mary's whose morals were stricter, then, maybe, she would get over her fear.

She found a peace of mind in this decision. That night she packed a suitcase. She slept soundly – the first time for ages. The next morning at four o'clock she left a note explaining why and left for her Aunt Mary's. To get over and remove all her fears of sex, she hoped. Oh! How hard she tried!

(Third-year girl)

3. The Ideal Mature Person: My Mother

My ideal mature person is my mother. I don't know that anyone could have a better mother than mine – I know that's what everyone thinks about their mother, but mine is sort of different.

She's not young and maybe that's why I respect her so much. If she was younger then I would treat her more as an equal instead of the person she really is, and in that way I wouldn't see her as the kind of person she is.

Ever since I was a child she has made me completely independent. She never fussed about whether I'd get across the main road all right or if I would cut my hand mowing the lawn or anything silly like most mums do. I was always encouraged to go on long journeys by myself, and when I was eight I went up to London completely alone. I think mature people always bring their children up to be independent. As life was a bit of a struggle for Mum she's not going to waste any time on her own children fussing about.

She's understanding as well and her judgement of people is rarely wrong. She likes to be confided in and also to have someone to confide in and that person is usually myself. Maybe she confides in me because she thinks she is bringing me up knowing that other people trust me and respect my opinion, but this is unlikely as I think she is the kind of person who needs someone to pour all her troubles on to otherwise she would go mad. Anyway, I don't mind because I like to feel I'm doing Mum a favour, and I think this is the main key to maturity – being so nice to people that they like to do you a favour. And that's where respect comes in.

I think the main reason why I respect my Mum is because I know she means what she says. When I was about three I remember being told that if I swore she would wash my mouth out with soap. Well, all child-like, I swore, and she kept her word. It was horrible! Then one day we went to the seaside and I was told that if I went far away I would be lost. As it happened I met a little boy (I was still only three) and played with him for hours running along the beach, and, of course, disobeying my mother. I landed up in a lost children's department of the police station and when Mum finally 'claimed' me there was none of this 'oh–my–poor–little–lost–child' nonsense, it was just 'well you've learnt your lesson, don't do it again'. It was through little incidents like this that I began to respect Mum at a very early age. I knew that she knew best and if I went against her word I was in for it.

Another thing I like about my Mum is that she lets everyone know exactly where they stand in a pleasant sort of way. She's the type who could get on with anyone although she may dislike them – but she never shows this.

Mum is always happy and hardly ever moans. She works hard to keep the house nice, but never slaves, as she says herself many women waste their lives over a kitchen sink, and life is so short its really not worth it. If she's tired she rests – she has learnt through experience not to slog on to the bitter end but to rest along the way and work is almost a pleasure. This is one of the things I have picked up from her.

Mum is always taking up new interests. She hasn't got a job as she says that she would prefer her children to grow up coming home to a nice warm house and the tea ready. Instead she interests herself in various hobbies – she has been to various classes in dress-making, cookery and typewriting and has taken and passed many exams. At the moment she has just passed her driving test and of course we are all thrilled. A mature person is one who realizes that life is very short so enjoys it to the full and doesn't waste time grubbing round at home all day.

Mum always keeps herself looking neat and attractive and dresses to her age, unlike many women who fancy themselves in a second adolescence.

She's an excellent listener, can hold a good conversation and always offers a logical solution to a problem. She is never flustered and rarely impatient. She lets us have an awful lot of freedom, so there are no secret romances, in fact everything is brought out into the open and I think this is the best way. She has always treated me as a person years older than my age and encouraged us in all our interests.

Parents, like teachers, are born, not made. So is your respect for them – it is automatic or else not at all. I think that I must be born lucky!

One thing that I consider most important is a good sense of humour. Although Mum hasn't got a quick wit she can certainly take a joke and would do anything for a laugh. She's the type to always get a party going – she's not domineering but she would inspire anyone to join in, she's a kind of driving force, and although she never makes herself noticeable or conspicuous, you're always conscious of her. In the face of an emergency she never panics but keeps her head. When she was learning to drive, if ever I went with her I felt completely at ease. Once she went out with her friend and the clutch went at the top of the hill and we started rolling back. It was during the cold weather when all the ice was on the road so she pulled on the handbrake and burst out laughing – until she realized we would have to push the car to the nearest garage.

She loves kids and can keep them occupied for hours. She never loses her temper and is always the perfect lady to everyone. In fact, I think my Mum is the ideal mature person.

(Third-year girl)

Society

1. The Law is Broken and so are You

Axis peers down from his scaffolding with accusing alabaster features.

'Fun in the bushes is not good for young girls not yet sixteen. Well it's not that, it's illegal you see.'

You have committed the treacherous crime of being a woman before your time. Your punishment is to be turned back into a girl, and when the Axis waves his magic wand, all will be as before.

The inquisition finds you guilty of acting naturally when everyone else acts unnaturally. Sex is only for people who are old enough not to enjoy it, and for whom it has no meaning.

We will send you away, excuse your actions as being due to a nervous breakdown, let you stay with 'relations' for a few months; then we let you loose with ball and chain of legal morality to prevent mother nature taking over again.

Please appreciate, we are doing this to protect you. If it drives you genuinely insane, don't blame us.

And remember —

Everything good which happens is through God's grace, and everything bad is your own fault.

(Sixth-form boy)

2. On the Run

No, I haven't been to jail, not yet anyway, I'm just being hunted, hunted for what I've done. I'll get this straight between you and me now, I'm not ashamed of anything, I'm not ashamed of killing that girl. . . .

I went up to the Youth Club a few weeks ago. There was a party on, quite a big thing. Anyhow, I was introduced to this girl about the same age as me. From the moment I met her, I don't know why, I hated her. She was a common little slut and everything she did got on my nerves. Later on that evening, I found out that she had pinched my guy. That night, I went round to her house, after the party, and asked her if, the next day, she would come over the fields with me for a walk – you know, I told her the boys would probably be there. She thought I was her friend. No, I was her worst enemy. I suppose you have guessed what happened. It was as easy as winking. When she turned round I knifed her. I didn't think I had killed her as it needed so little effort on my part. . . .

I didn't dare go back home. I was prepared not to. Everyone knew that I was going out with her alone and if I came back all by myself they would start wondering what had happened. At the moment I'm just wondering what to do. Every movement or sound makes me jump. I have no food, just a five-pound note. I can't go into the city as some-one might recognize me but I can't go on without food.

Just lately I have found out that one crime leads to another. Last night I slept out in the open and I was terrified. An owl flew through one of the trees nearby. I wanted to scream but I couldn't. I was too scared to scream, besides I couldn't afford to be heard. I was so terrified I had to run, run to get rid of some of my fears. I came to a farmhouse. The dog started barking so I became very still and tried to be quiet but I nearly started crying. The dog stopped barking and I crept up to the farm kitchen (the dog was round the other side of the farm). I knew how to break in quietly. You have to keep pressing all the way round the window-frame and the glass will become loose. The windows were quite old and they were easy to take out.

I climbed into the kitchen. It was very dark. I could see a lot of weird shapes. From one corner of the room I heard a big clock ticking very slowly. I was cold, tired and hungry and very much afraid. I suppose you will think me silly, but for one second I imagined I heard Susan's voice. She's the girl I murdered. I can tell you, I nearly fainted with fright. I told myself not to be so daft and then I felt that horrible feeling that comes over you when you know you have no one to turn to, nowhere to go and nothing to live for. I felt I was just being hunted, like an animal, but that's what I treated Susan like.

I stole all the food I could find. I was glad to get out of the place. All I could find, though, was one tin of biscuits. The next morning I went near the village, hoping no one would recognize me. I felt very near to suicide but I just couldn't bring myself to it. Strange isn't it that I can just kill someone straight off and yet be too scared to kill myself?

I went past a shop which sold newspapers. Splashed all over the front page I read 'Police Seek Killer of Teenage Girl' and underneath there was a photograph of me. I knew the police would be after me soon, but I hadn't realized how soon! I went back over the fields wondering what to do. I doubt if my parents would have helped me. I doubt if they will help me now, so I think I'm going to give myself up. I must escape from this feeling of being hunted, no peace, no rest until I know I am forgiven. No one will forgive me though, not even this 'God' they talk of. No, my life is not worth living any more. It is worse than being in jail; in jail you know you deserve all you get. You are being punished. On the run you are in your own prison, only you know you deserve a much harder punishment, a much harder jail.

(Third-year girl)

3. In Hospital

I looked out of the window of the small sunlit room. A grass verge extended for about a hundred yards and then my view was obstructed by a large brick wall – a characteristic symbol to those outside. Soon I would be outside that wall.

I cannot say they were unkind to me here, on the contrary, they were too kind. Those sweet, hypocritical smiles used to encourage me, now they make me laugh – these are their very special smiles, put on for our benefit, used to segregate us from humanity and to hide their apprehensive feelings. And they are apprehensive you can tell that by the way they humour us, treat us like children in the hope of subduing our 'highly emotional psychology' as they call it.

And then there were the whispers – always whispers. They mutter concernedly to one another and develop a false, sickly cheerful, front when acknowledging us. As we are different from the rest of humanity we must be partitioned off and treated differently, but how can they restore us to our senses when they treat us like idiots? How can they know what is going on in our minds by merely summing up our external symptoms?

But soon I will have quitted this place. Soon I shall meet people again – not parts of people. Visitors were rare, and those who came were embarrassed as to what they should say and how we might react. People are inwardly nervous and cower when they meet us, and yet will mock and joke about us when amongst friends.

It is quiet here; I shall miss the peace. Quiet, that is, except for the occasional scream or hysterical laugh, and of course, the whispering – but these I have grown accustomed to. Worldly noises have almost been forgotten.

My mind and body feel relaxed and peaceful now after the stormy struggle of mixed emotions and despondent confusion. It had been a difficult and slow fight, joining my disordered life, piece by piece, until eventually a clear picture was formed. I had succeeded in doing this – not them. They assume they can, but they cannot comprehend our feelings. Their only useful treatment which they could give to me was peace and time – the rest I had to work out for myself.

The rhythmic squeak of shoes on a polished floor returned me to the present. A man in a white coat entered, bringing with him his familiar grin which had become automatic but which he need not use on me now. I took one last look at the room – it was luxury compared with

93

the bare isolation cells of the majority here. I had a handle on my door, and glass at the window, and a mirror on the wall.

And now, at last, I am to leave into a world which has become a stranger. Will I be accepted into their world? I think not. There will still be the understanding whispers and pointing fingers, the giggles from children, and the artificial humouring and the exaggerated sweetness from adults. They will still have their suspicions and doubts which I hope will relax when I show them how I can talk like them, and do not stamp or rave or grind my teeth.

They shut me away because I was upsetting their smooth patterned way of life, but I feel I have surpassed them now because I have experienced life and found a meaning whilst they still grovel, hopelessly on, accepting life as it comes and hardly daring to question it.

(Fifth-year girl)

4. Hiroshima

Wars are terrible things,
Blood is as frequent as water,
People are made homeless,
Their houses ruined by bombs,
Hundreds of people are killed every day.
The world is a ball of fire.
I hate wars and wars seem to hate me and everything of joy.

Atomic War

Once it was a city, now it is wasteland.
All that remains are a few burnt out houses.
A handful of scraggly birds are flying overhead.
They are looking for any scraps of food that may be left.
Starved and ragged are the people.
They trudge on to find new homes.
Many are dead and have to be buried
But for those alive it is the biggest tragedy ever.

(First-year girls)

5. Escapism

(written after seeing *The War Game*)

I cannot turn but see
a child with an old man's head
I cannot wake but hear
the cries of weeping mothers
I cannot run but find
the ruin of a burnt-out home.

I cannot look on this world any more,
I do not accept it.

I run into my garden
where the flowers grow and the birds sing
where the stream trickles lazily over coloured stones.
I am safe here.
The sun smiles down at me
filling my aching body with warmth,
causing me to lie down on the carpet of petals,
safe in my garden . . .
I want to stay here always.
But as I lie beneath my sheltering tree
the blackness that I left outside slowly creeps in
through the grass
around the great trees
over the smooth ground
enveloping everything with black venom.

Still I lie here,
watching a white rose
as the heavy black liquid creeps over its petals
making them sag
then drips off the end of each one
onto my outstretched hands.

It stings me.
It burns my flesh:
I spring up but too late —
the liquid, black as night, black as hate,
slowly envelops my writhing body
slowly enters my unbelieving mind.

(Sixth-form girl)

96

6. Life through Frustrated Eyes

I work in the rice fields all day through;
I am only a peasant, a poor Vietnamese.
They bomb us with napalm,
They fire our homes,
They destroy the jungle
Just to please their egoistic minds.
But our life still goes on.
It must go on, or we will die —
Die from starvation, die of thirst.
We must reap a harvest
From our battered land.
We must make do with what is left.
After the Americans have mutilated it.
The Americans – the slick-talking Americans,
They bandage our wounds to create others.
They say they are doing it for us,
Doing what? Destroying our lives.
They destroy our lives for us.
The war is against the North, not us.
Oh how I wish they would go,
Go back to America and leave us alone.
Leave us to live our lives in peace,
Leave us to live and not to die.

(Fourth-year boy)

97

Religion

1. The Truth Hurts like the Fire Burns

I am cold and frozen and set in my ways.
Go away!
Don't disturb me.
I am asleep and dead to everything.
I am too deaf to hear you,

Too blind to see you.
I am set in my ways,
Frozen,
Stiff.
Don't blow your scorching breath to melt away my skin.
Don't disturb me truth!

Go away realism!
Don't break my barrier,
Smelt my dreams.
Don't penetrate my frozen face
For I am afraid you will find nothing behind!
Not even a skeleton.

(Fourth-year girl)

2. The Man who Died

Slowly, very slowly
He moved towards the door.
Then he winced back;
The blinding sun had struck its blow.
At last he put his foot out;
The soft springy grass tickled the sole of his foot.

The birds sang,
The smell of sweet fresh flowers,
The deafening din of the people in the market,
The heat of the sun
Feeling and sensing the light breeze blowing gently on his face.

No more blackness,
No more darkness,
No more silence.

(First-year boy)

3. A-New

As if a Rip Van Winkle
As if a new born child.
Three days in a wilderness
Three days in perpetual darkness.
More like an interrogation as the sun blazes down,
Let me go to my paradise.
My feet give immense pain
Pain as if an immortal wound.
My eyes do not accept the light,
Everything is a-haze,
As if looking through murky water.
I feel sick with hunger
No food, not a morsel.
My throat is dry.
I feel giddy.
I fall to the ground.

(First-year boy)

4. Into a Paradise of Colours

Out! Out!
Stepping into a known but different world
Then dazzling dazzling colours.
His eyes close
Then he peeps out above his defensive arms.
Still shielding his eyes he peers around.
The world seems to be turning and swirling.
He stops!
And sits down to rest.
The world seems so colourful now.
The world seems different!
More like a Paradise of Colours.
More like a box of paints.
Just to think he had taken it all for granted!

(First-year girl)

5

In my church
On the wall
Hangs a cross
Great & tall
Symbol of the King who died
For the world of sin he tried
To save our souls from evil
Jesus Son of God was He
Kind & Loving
Pure in heart
And we best
Can do our part
To serve him both
With hand & heart

(First-year girl)

6. The Feast of the Sun

The Sun will come again, after the Winter.
Its martyrdom is in the Autumn
And its resurrection is in the Spring.
Its rebirth is so that the Earth will live again.

In the days when the world was young
The people would sacrifice at the Feast of the Sun
And the price of its resurrection was blood.
The people needed a symbol that death was not the end.

Have we come so far?
Now instead of the Sun we have a Jewish prophet.

(Fifth-year boy)

7. The Importance of Going to Church

Part 1

You must wear a hat
It doesn't matter if you don't believe
You can't wear trousers
But you must wear a hat.
It's more important what you wear
Than why you go
And for goodness' sake
When the priest prays
Look as if you are praying too.
I don't care if you read a book
As long as the neighbours don't see
And whatever you do
Do it quietly
Please don't sing too loud
Mrs Jones likes to be heard
And if you sing above her
She's liable to walk out —
Oh, and don't forget what I said
You must wear a hat.

Part 2

You must wear a hat. The most important part of going to church!
Damn you if you want to honour your God – just make sure that you
are dressed correctly and you don't offend Mrs Jones by singing too
loud! Oh don't be so pathetic – bring yourselves alive. Christ meant
you to help people, all the time – people who are repulsive and who
will never thank you. Don't be a one-day Christian – because if you
are, you are not a Christian – my friend you are a hypocrite. Action is a
Christian, action seven days a week, 365 days a year, not rows of well-
dressed old ladies in beige straw hats sitting in pews on a Sunday. Put
your money into the collecting plate and make sure that Mrs Brown
sees you put ten shillings in! Dear God – save these people, your people
from becoming mummified beings – goad them into action or your
world will fail – too soon.

(Sixth-form girl)

Death

The dust flew up and caught my face and hair. I walked slowly; the black veil flickered and drifted across my eyes. A wooden giant loomed before me towards a hollow, an empty hole. The sky blackened, and a fine misty drizzle was swept by the wind across the graveyard. We still moved on, like a snake, slowly sliding towards its prey. The procession halted, and carefully the wooden box was lifted down, and lowered into the cavity, the empty cavity.

As she lay there, below me, a few flowers fell from white, shaking hands. Then it began. A shovel of earth spattered across the top of the lid. Another. She was leaving me. My face was wet with tears and rain. Farther and farther, with each shovel, smaller and smaller. I turned my head and slowly walked away, but I couldn't. I had to go back to her. I fell on my knees and my tears ran into the earth where she lay.

A hand took my arm and led me away, but I still screamed for her. How could I ever show them what she meant to me? What is she now? She was my mother. But what is she now?

(Fifth-year girl)

2. One Man's Death

He could hear the murmured sentences curving round his bed, the overlying grief covering the underlying relief that this rich old fool was nearly dead. Every now and then that pretty young nurse would feel his wrist and a soft 'not yet' would circulate. He thought he could feel his body growing numb, detached and dead. He listened to the old heart pumping the thin blood round; he could sense the slight rocking of the bed in response to his pulse. The heart faltered and he felt rich warm pain coursing his body; it faltered again and stopped. For the first time he realized what the heart meant to a body, it was its motor, its being, and now he felt empty and lost, a patter of human thought in an already cooling body. He felt himself drawing away as someone lifted the sheet up over the pale head. He heard the cynical whispering as the small group left the room; no, he didn't hear it, he sensed it. It all seemed perfectly natural as the scene faded from his senses; he felt no panic, no remorse; he had got rid of that earthbound body and now – and now what? There was nothing but blackness all round him and silence, an explosive silence, but of course he now had no sight or hearing or touch; the blackness was his own unknowing. There would be no more human afflictions, no pain, no exhaustion, just floating in the warm black and thought. Thought, he must now be composed of pure thought, unseeing, unfeeling, unbeing, just suspended in nothingness after leaving its trapped existence in the human body. Why, with infinity in front of him he could solve all the problems that had nagged all his life, but he had never had the time to figure them out; now he had all the time in the world. The problems came and went, solved and passed, but never to be applied. He began to feel bored and this scared him, because boredom was the only but the ultimate pain he could suffer. A few times he perceived mental holes opening up before him but he had not the power to enter them. He thought these must be crude efforts by humans to contact the spirits, but the power was never large enough, as only a few believed.

Then he began to feel tuggings at his mind, he began to sense falling and buffeting. He felt something was happening; perhaps this was the next stage of his being. He began to feel pain, he felt trapped, he felt warm. The pain was building up until he wanted to writhe with agony. Then the crushing came: it hit him and constricted him: he suddenly felt suffocated and then he was free. The air burnt its way down to his damp shrivelled lungs and he screamed, so that his little body shook, and then the mental shroud dropped and he was gone.

106

The young man in the neat dark suit carefully opened the door and closed it softly behind him. The room smelt of antiseptic and talcum powder, as the rest of the wing did, and his shoes squeaked on the well-worn linoleum as he walked up to the bed in the centre. His wife lay on the bed holding a small pink body with a few wisps of blond hair on its little head.

'What did the doctor say?' she asked, looking up.

'Oh, he says you can return home in a couple of days, as Mum said she would look after you; how's my little son coming along? Anyway, he still looks the same to me.'

'He's doing fine, but I'm surprised you don't see the difference. For the first couple of days he looked just like an old man, just like my grandfather who died two years ago, but now he's filling out and is beginning to look like an ordinary plump baby.'

(Fifth-year boy)

3. Childhood Fears

Lynette stands on her bed and stares out of the window. The wind is buffeting the trees so that the street lights wink on and off. It's dark but not quiet. The blustery movement relaxes her like the darting flames of a bright fire. Standing in the darkness of the bedroom she is secure, not from the heaving wind but from her father's stormy temper. The death of her mother leaves her free to float about in her own dreams, instead of being endlessly dragged back to reality. She loved her mother, understand, but she has not cried. Why? Who knows, maybe because her mother, being a typical person, could never exist in her world. She was always complaining about the weather. Her washing would get wet. She hated fog. Lynette hopes its foggy tomorrow. Let the wind bring all the fog from London and Scotland to blanket the cemetery. Lynette hates graves. The gaping hole stares up at you, never blinking, and sucks you down into the earth. You cling to the edge, but it has your feet. You can't help yourself. You're caught like a spider in the vacuum cleaner, sucked in under the houses and sea. Everyone is there. You can't be alone. There's no wind, not even any fog to provide you with your own cubicle-world. She'll be happy down there, to do her washing and never a spot of rain.

God please don't let me die, please, please don't let me die. When I get old, can't I just start again? Please don't let me die. Let me jump backwards like on Television.

(Fifth-year girl)

4. Two Image Poems: Life and Death

Birth is like a balloon,
Suddenly being blown up into a new sphere,
And then let go one dawn
It sails towards a thorn!
Bang!
Death has come.

I put my sky rocket in a bottle,
And then light it with a match.
Suddenly whoosh! Sparks fly,
As it soars up into the dark sky
And then – death! It breaks up
Sending red stars back to earth.

(First-year boy)

5. Death is the Answer to my Prayer

My prayer is simple:
I pray for the powers of the night,
For the intelligent souls long dead,
Peace for the dying who are learning the truth,
Life for the dead who have learnt the truth
And death for the living who pretend to know the truth.
If you want to know the divine truth,
You must die.
How many people want to know the truth and are not prepared
  to die?

(Fourth-year girl)

Four

'It could be said that the advances of reason have constituted a continual
encroachment on the world of symbols, reducing their numbers one by
one . . . Symbols are not just an imaginative framework: they are able
to release a considerable amount of potential psychic energy and
Jung has shown that the role of symbols with regard to energy is that of
real transformers, a sort of bridge which allows psychic energy to pass
from one level to another; they should allow consciousness to realize what
Jung has called the transcendant function of the psyche, that is to say the
approach and conciliation in the human being of the rational and
irrational, the harmonizing and unification of contraries.'[47]

It was towards the end of the Easter term and I decided that I would
do some work with my fifth form based on the Crucifixion. The only
difficulty would be to bring it alive. The Crucifixion has become an
object of belief or non-belief in our society and I wanted to go beneath
this to what is permanent in the Crucifixion. I wanted to break through
the conventional to the symbolic. In no way did I want to touch upon
dogma. Let it be irrelevant whether Jesus was Divine or Human! He
was a man pierced with nails to the cross – suffering man. This was more
than enough! The crucifix – the killing of man by man – pathetic,
absurd. The Crucifixion had to be presented as permanently real to man
– as Grunewald had presented it in his vision. The pupil's religious dis-
position did not matter – such experience could not be evaded.

In Anne Sexton's poem I found, partly, what I was looking for. In
the poem, the suffering is extended to include that of the poet: both
are lost, incapable of making judgements, in a wilderness of what
appears pointless torment.

For God While Sleeping

Sleeping in fever, I am unfit
to know just who you are:
hung up like a pig on exhibit,
the delicate wrists,
the beard drooling blood and vinegar;
hooked to your own weight,
jolting toward death under your nameplate.

Everyone in this crowd needs a bath.
I am dressed in rags.

The mother wears blue. You grind your teeth
and with each new breath
your jaws gape and your diaper sags.
I am not to blame
for all this. I do not know your name.

Skinny man, you are somebody's fault.
You ride on dark poles —
a wooden bird that a trader built
for some fool who felt
that he could make the flight. Now you roll
in your sleep, seasick
on your own breathing, poor old convict.[48]

I liked the poem too for its starkness, its brutal honesty. Too many artists have placed a beautiful young boy on the Cross – and *idealized* what must have been the torment of the man.

Even so I wanted a greater circumference than that presented by the Anne Sexton poem. I wanted the extension of suffering, beyond this man, this writer, to the world at large. Wherever there is suffering – there is crucifixion. It might be in concentration camps, in Harlem, in South Africa, in one's own country, suburb, among one's friends, one's family, or in oneself. Perhaps I would have to talk about this opening up – but then, I remembered Ted Walker's 'Easter Day'. This poem made the extension from man to nature: from Christ to the fox stretched and nailed on the barn door.

Easter Day

I had gone on Easter Day
early and alone to be
beyond insidious bells
(that any other Sunday
I'd not hear) up to the hills
where are winds to blow away

commination. In the frail
first light I saw him, unreal
and sudden through lifting mist,
a fox on a barn door, nailed
like a coloured plaster Christ
in a Spanish shrine, his tail

coiled around his loins. Sideways
his head hung limply, his ears
snagged with burdock, his dry nose

112

plugged with black blood. For two days
he'd held the orthodox pose.
The endemic English noise

of Easter Sunday morning
was mixed in the mist swirling
and might have moved his stiff head.
Under the hill the ringing
had begun: and the sun rose red
on the stains of his bleeding.

I walked the length of the day's
obsession. At dusk I was
swallowed by the misted barn,
sucked by the peristalsis
of my fear that he had gone,
leaving nails for souvenirs.

But he was there still. I saw
no sign. He hung as before.
Only the wind had risen
to comb the thorns from his fur.
I left my superstition
stretched on the banging barn door.[49]

Like the Anne Sexton, this poem had a visual starkness – an insistence
on keeping the experience honest, a refusal to idealize. And yet neither
is there indulgence. The two poems do not deteriorate into a Ginsberg
scream.

The fox must have reminded me of R. S. Thomas's poem.

The fox drags its wounded belly
Over the snow, the crimson seeds
Of blood burst with a mild explosion,
Soft as excrement, bold as roses.

Over the snow that feels no pity,
Whose white hands can give no healing,
The fox drags its wounded belly.[50]

Here, dramatically, simply, R. S. Thomas succeeds in evoking pure
suffering. There is no mention of crucifixion and yet it is just this. This
was the point at which I wanted to arrive in the class-room situation.
From that point, I hoped, the pupils could write directly about the
Crucifixion – working from whatever experience they felt compelled
to.

I opened the lesson with this reading from the Gospel of St Mark which somehow seems to emphasize the appalling indifference of the people, the appalling despair of the man, whose mission was one of love:

And with him they crucify two thieves; the one on his right hand, and the other on his left. And the scripture was fulfilled, which saith, 'And he was numbered with the transgressors.'

And they that passed by railed on him, wagging their heads, and saying, 'Ah, thou that destroyest the temple, and buildest it in three days, save thyself, and come down from the cross.'

Likewise also the chief priests mocking said among themselves with the scribes, 'He saved others; himself he cannot save. Let Christ the King of Israel descend now from the cross that we may see and believe.'

And they that were crucified with him reviled him.

And when the sixth hour was come, there was darkness over the whole land until the ninth hour.

And at the ninth hour Jesus cried with a loud voice, saying, 'Eloi, Eloi, lama sabacthani?' which is, being interpreted,

'My God, my God, why hast thou forsaken me?'

And some of them that stood by, when they heard it, said, 'Behold, he calleth Elias.' And one ran and filled a sponge full of vinegar, and put it on a reed and gave him to drink, saying, 'Let alone; let us see whether Elias will come to take him down.'

And Jesus cried with a loud voice and gave up the ghost.

And the veil of the temple was rent in twain from the top to the bottom. And when the centurion, which stood over against him saw that he so cried out, and gave up the ghost, he said, 'Truly this man was the Son of God.'

After reading the passage I commented on the last sigh of Christ, 'My God, my God, why hast thou forsaken me?' Did it all end here? In utter defeat? The question opened the way into the Anne Sexton's 'For God While Sleeping'. I suggested that the title indicated both the poet's disturbed unknowing state and that of God, who appeared completely absent, asleep. Then I read the poem. And with brief connecting comments moved into the two fox poems. The Crucifixion was a symbol of all suffering, in the past, now and to come. They could write about Good Friday as they felt impelled to. They could hand it in when they felt ready to in whatever form they wished.

Here is the work that was handed in. I will leave the reader to judge for himself the quality of the individual pieces, but I contend that, taken as a whole, the work shows a real diversity in response together with an energetic use of forms. The actual lesson was given some time after the work described in Chapters Two and Three had been done and I think one can see the results of this work particularly in the imaginative freedom that the writing displays.

It also seems right that I should conclude this section on creative writing by showing all* the work handed in. The reader can then see how the pupils using different powers of expression and understanding have attempted to define a fundamental experience.

* There were 22 pupils in this particular class. One girl decided that her work was not good enough to hand in – a situation that the teacher must be ready to accept with this sort of work. One boy's work I have, unfortunately misplaced. The class was the second of five Fifth-year English sets in a Grammar School that served, in the main, a lower middle-class suburb.

1. The Crucifixion

Blood and wood mingled in cruelty
Stained flesh punctured and torn and hung up like meat.
A man's face, distorted in agony and despair
And hair lank and moist.

Naked limbs, streaked scarlet, and stretched
In the shape 'symbolizing suffering'
Men gazing, laughing, sneering,
'It's none of our business.'

A stiff, winced movement
Parched lips mould a stifled word,
And form a broken sentence.
'Quick, give him vinegar.'

A rigid corpse, peace at last.
The crowd dwindle pathetically away.
They heard his words and saw him dead,
And they will crucify another day.

(Janette)

2. The 'Other'

Riddled with bullets, tied by the feet, and there
for people to mock and scorn,
Hung Mussolini and his mistress, side by side
from an erected network of wooden bars.
From the metal opened holes had trickled blood –
bright red blood. Now it was dark and dried –
just like their lives.
His face was bloody and it still held the deep
lines of cruelty and, maybe even pain.
He'd done wrong, tortured many and he had
been cruel —
But now he hung upside-down in the sunlit square.
Gazing at the shadow on the scorched earth,
I was reminded of 'another',
Another, who had died hanging from wooden bars,
Bars in the ugly shape of a cross.
He too had had someone by his side – two common
convicts – one either side of Him, and there was
also one other whom no one saw.
This man had done no wrong – He had done
wonderful things; He had given help, restored
many to health. He had loved – but had not been
equally loved.
People had been overjoyed at seeing Mussolini
hanging – The feeling seemed to have differed
little for the 'other'.
That time, it was no rope that had held Him tied
to the wooden bars – instead large nails had kept
Him in place.
His body had not been riddled with bullets – but
instead, a sword had been thrust into His side.
Thorns had pierced His brow.
I had seen Mussolini's torture as he hung.
I had not seen the 'Other's' – But now I understood
how much He must have suffered, how much He
quietly bore.
But there was even a greater difference – Mussolini
was hung facing hell, the 'Other' was facing heaven.

(Sandra)

117

3. *The King*

The man must die to cleanse the people.
The suffering is the redemption.
That is the ancient mythology.
For us all there must be a scapegoat,
The Man, the King, the God.
Is there not reality in that?
Is there not even the husk of
    greatness in that?
Do you not see?
The Man becomes the King and the
God through suffering.
The suffering is the redemption.

                                     (Nicholas)

        the cross –
hope   glory Agony Death
God   truth   now?   when?
Never gone   coming soon
hope   love   peace   hate
yes   no   where? when?
forced argued accepted dismissed
        Oh God
for the love of God for Christ's sake
in the name of God the Father
And God the son believe in
        heaven
        hell
   eternal life
and die happily to lie under soil
        and stones
               because that's
the end

                  (Heather)

5. Pain

So great an animal   is the elephant   that
it has the right   of being called   the
greatest living animal
    but
his immense size and power stops not   the pain
    made by a simple thin piece   of wire
    no longer than a yard
       this unsuspecting animal treads its
path through harmless foragery
    but then
    an obstruction is felt   his foot is being
restricted from movement
    in his massive heavy skull   is a brain
    no larger than a melon
it's not enough   to explain this increasing pain
    using his strength   which solved
most previous problems   he tries to wrench
himself free   but   to no advantage
    the wire tightens   and cuts deeply into
his thickleatherskin   there is no
    way to loosen it   no relief from pain
    except
DEATH   slowly the wound
    begins to swell   finally the
wire reaches the bone   now all hope is
    lost   all he can wait for
is   the soothing   relaxation   of
      death.

(Peter)

6

Now I am alone
Where are my followers
Those I healed —
The lepers,
The lame,
The deaf,
The dumb?
Those in need
Whom I helped,
Have deserted me
In my hour of need.
I came to help —
Not to destroy.
But you cruel men
Are destroying me
And turning a blind eye
To all my teaching.
I am crucified
Like an animal.
Even my father
Has deserted me —
Yet I forgive and forget.

(Jennifer)

7. Fox the Hunter

Stealthily the fox crept,
padding quietly along its way,
the thick carpet of pine needles,
giving no warning crack as he went.
The long shadows of the night
hiding all but the fleeting glimpse of teeth – white.
See the tip of the long nose
quivering to the hunt.

Somewhere in front, stoat stirred,
edged on by a primeval sense
of danger – akin to all animals.
So slyly – stoat slid along,
belly edging towards its lair.

Behind – fox picked up the spoor,
and the pad-pad of paws on earth
quickened – as did the tremors of
                              its body,
heavy jowl's edging back
to bare teeth
              sharp!

At the call of night owl
fox met stoat —
stoat transfixed in its terror
                    unmoving
Jaws of the fox slowly —
      with saliva
            dripping.

Suddenly!
    stoat broke from the terrible gaze
                          and fled.
Fox growled
and long-lean haunches —
moving with easy grace,
                  followed.
Hunter and hunted.
Moon giving silent watch – with cold stare,

Both ran, one for the living
one for the dead.

Fox stopped,
his jaws open'd with screech
              of pain
hind leg caught in metal jaws,
screaming body – leaping high,
blood of fox – flowing
              freely.
Slowly – painfully – fox stiffens
              in tortured pain.
Stoat slowly returns – to watch
with unblinking eyes, gloating
both in fear and surprise.
Slathering jaws – foam flecked —
lay fixed, immovable,
cold brown eye – cruel and staring,
stoat watches and quietly leaves.

Moon moves – silently over the
long grey shadow – lying so still.

                                   (Martin)

8. Death

Life,
   Like the spider's web,
Is tenuous and short,
    And death
Is but a hair's breadth away.
Death secures its victim,
    And locks it,
To an incomprehensible future,
   A future,
Ruled by immaterial beings,
    The supernatural
And to a void
   That can be explored
   Throughout the rest of eternity,
As the bodiless souls,
   Float on,
     Unthinking,
       Unknowing,
What,   Is to come.

(Colin)

9. Ten Minutes of Blood and Dust

Bloody money,
Pays for his death.
A ten minute struggle
In the scorching sun:
And he dies.
A victim of the modern world,
Killed for people's pleasure.
Tormented by the matador,
Enraged by the crowd,
In the dust of the arena,
He makes his final stand,
Against humanity.
In ten minutes or ten hours,
Time is no barrier.
His blood paints the words
On his gravestone of dust:
Words that will be changed
When the next bull dies.

(Clive)

Look at them, look at their faces
Oh, God they hate me.
Everything I did for them is
Lost and forgotten.
Why did they forget?
They nail'd me here
To me they gave the punishment
Of a murderer.
But this hill would never hold
All the crosses,
On which should hang those who
Murdered me.
The time is too close
These hot waves of pain
Which surpass the torture of
My ripping hands.
People! Into your hands I
Commend my spirit.

(Mary)

11. *The Operation*

I lay still, my body resisting
any form of movement,
Eyes staring down at me –
cold and hard
I felt the pain in my wrist
The figures appeared ghostly
And were then devoured by the darkness.
Darkness – it means so much yet
it is nothing
And – as the velvety blackness
surrounded me I felt . . .
I was somewhere yet knew I was nowhere.
My senses were non-existent
No pain
or vision – but I was aware
of my presence.
There was no longer any time.
Was now for ever?
Had I reached eternity?
But light slowly overcame the darkness –
and I was faced once more with reality.
I was alive, but for a while
had my mind travelled elsewhere?
or my soul?

(Diane)

'Paul's a dirty rotten creep!'

'Paul's a dirty rotten creep!'

Their childish, mocking voices sang with a shrill cruelty, and a heavy, choking lump blocked his throat so that he couldn't swallow.

A quick foot jerked forward and neatly kicked his shins. The blow was sharp, and painful.

Someone else banged heavily against him. His foot slipped and he lost his balance. The world spun round, and the voices behind him suddenly became scared.

Someone shouted, 'He's falling off the edge!' but it was too late and each of the boys turned with a sick feeling beating in his stomach and ran crazily away.

Paul fell, and his arms went wild, waving and clutching at nothing as it swished past his ears. Then his finger-nails ripped on something cold and hard, and his fingers clawed and scrabbled desperately at the solidity. The solidity crumbled, and screams twisted and distorted his face as, for a few seconds, he fought like a lunatic against gravity. Then, as the solidity became dust, his writhing body suddenly became still, and dropped like a stone on to the rocks below, where the sea washed the blood from wounds in his hands and side, forming streaks, which crossed in the water, like a crucifix.

(Rosemary)

13. The Spider

Cathy sat on the floor of her playroom, holding a teddy bear, her other toys littered all around her.

Suddenly she caught sight of a spider scurrying across the floor. She picked up an empty box, and, turning it upside-down, trapped the spider under it.

'Now I've got you,' she whispered. 'What are you going to do now?' Cathy slowly lifted the box and placed her hand on the floor beside the spider. It climbed on to it. She held it in her cupped hands. It lay motionless. She blew on it – it jumped and tickled her hands. Half-amused, half-frightened, Cathy dropped the spider and stood up, unconsciously rubbing the palms of her hands on her skirt to rid herself of the feel of the insect. It scurried away into the nearest corner. Cathy looked round for something to poke it out with. She found an old knitting-needle and used that. The spider came out, cautiously moved an inch or two, then a bit more, blind to its attacker. Cathy smiled. She held its life in her grasp, and it was powerless to stop her killing it.

Suddenly the spider darted towards her. Cathy jumped up, afraid. She bent down and stabbed at it with the needle. It squirmed and turned over on its back. She watched its legs wriggling about in the air. She laughed, amused by its helplessness. Then she crouched down to watch it. The spider writhed in agony; Cathy could almost hear it cry out. Then suddenly it stopped. She poked it with the needle. Slowly and pitifully its legs pawed the air.

Cathy suddenly felt ashamed. She was torturing this insect, who suddenly seemed like a real person, seeing and understanding everything that was going on, but unable to do anything about it. Cathy took one more look at the squirming body, and then picked up the box, turned it sideways and pressed it on to the spider. She heard it crunch, and a yellow liquid oozed out from under the box. She lifted it, and wrinkled her nose at the mess she had made.

'That was a real live animal a minute ago,' she thought, 'and I tortured it and killed it.'

She stood up quickly, and tried to rub away the evidence on the floor with her shoe; then she wiped the box with a rag. Hot, salty tears ran down her cheeks and into the corners of her mouth. She felt frightened and ashamed.

Cathy turned round and picked up her teddy bear. She held him close to her. She kissed his black woollen nose, fingered his funny ragged ears. Then she sat down and began to play with him.

(Patricia)

14

I lay quietly between the stiff white sheets, my eyes closed, listening. The smell of antiseptic tickled my nose. Voices hummed around me. My legs felt numb, my hands and arms heavy and insensible. My brain was muddled, my thoughts tangled incomprehensibly. I felt myself being pulled into the darkness of sleep, I relaxed and slept.

When I woke, darkness still surrounded me. The sheets had disappeared, underneath me the surface was hard and damp. The air was musty and dank and I felt as though I was shut up in a very small space. Behind me something moved. I wriggled closer to it, it was warm and soft. Other shapes kicked and struggled nearer as well. Another warm, soft object came towards me. It made a funny kind of panting noise and the ground trembled when it flopped down beside me. I felt happy and contented. I slept again.

(Penny)

15

The wet pavement glistened under the street lamps and a harsh wind whistled through the telegraph wires. Johnnie pulled up his coat collar to keep out some of the cold. It was late at night and not much traffic was around but as Johnnie crossed the road, the unexpected happened. The headlights glared in his face and the scream of tortured rubber filled his ears. The car hit Johnnie with a sickening thud and he felt his body crumple on impact.

When he regained consciousness, he was in a small white room, smelling of disinfectant. He had a peculiar feeling, as if his body was miles away. The doctors diagnosed multiple fractures of both legs and ribs, and severe brain damage. They sent out a description of Johnnie on radio and television, but no one seemed to want him. Johnnie was completely helpless and did not even notice the injections and pills that were given him.

Four days after entering hospital, he again lost consciousness and this time he never woke up. No one ever claimed him and so Johnnie died with his name unknown. The only two people who he trusted and loved had deserted him and left him to die because he was different to them.

(Michael)

16. Guilt

He rose, the knife in his hand, still wet with blood. Gina lay dead on the floor, her sightless eyes gazing up at him and her silent mouth wide in the shock of sudden death.

As he looked at her waves of guilt and nausea engulfed him and he stumbled out of the house and into his car. For a moment he waited while he regained control of his trembling body then he started the car and drove off, he didn't care where, he just wanted to get away. The road was empty and silent but for the drone of the engine as the car streaked past trees and bushes. For miles he drove and saw no one which seemed strange to him because it was hot and dry. He began to wonder why no one was about.

He stopped the car, it was quiet, no birds sang, no cars passed his, nothing moved.

The silence made him feel uneasy. He stood by the car and looked all around him, but not even a breeze rustled the summer leaves. He was quite alone.

Feeling more than a little apprehensive he got back into the car and switched on the radio. Nothing! Frantically he wrenched the tuning knob round and round but no sound came.

Waves of fear crept up his body and every nerve jumped with sudden panic. He started the car again and was relieved that that, at least, made a sound.

He drove for miles in utter isolation seeing no people and no signs of life. He was alone with his guilt, he was a killer and he and his conscience were alone in the universe.

The thought made him cringe. He stopped and got out of the car. He could hear something. The sea! There were bound to be people there on a hot summer day. He ran eagerly smiling like a child on a birthday, to the edge of the cliff. He stopped and looked down. Nothing. And even the tide going out to deprive him of its company.

'It's because I killed,' he thought, fingering the St Christopher which he always wore round his neck.

'I've got the mark of Cain on me.'

Feeling suddenly helpless and desolate he screamed hysterically, clutching his hands to his ears to shut out the ringing silence.

'Where are all the people?'

He fell on his face at the edge of the cliff and looked down.

The rocks below seemed to beckon him.

'Come on, jump, at least there'll be company in hell, jump! Jump!
So he stood up and let himself fall . . .
And as he fell he heard a woman scream.

(Jane)

Jim was a boy who didn't know what to think of religion – he didn't go to church, thought it was boring. His Scripture teacher was always going on about how Christ said that people should love their enemies, and how it would stop wars. During one of these lessons, Jim started to wonder what Christ was like. He had been told, as a child, that Christ lived up in the sky, but he soon rejected the idea as stupid.

He wondered if Christ could look down from up there what He would think of wars and the suffering they brought. Everything was a complete reversal of His teaching. Would He wonder if it had been worth while? Would He think He had given up a long, happy family life for nothing? Any ordinary man would wonder why, after His sacrifice, the people had taken no notice of what He taught. Would He decide that He died so that His teaching would be thought about but not practised? Of course, a few people practised it, but they were a minority – many people either knew nothing about Him or did not want to know about Him.

But no ordinary man could have stood the pain of His death and His degradation, except a fictional hero. But this was real! At least, if you believed what the Bible said. He was said to be no ordinary man – He was said to be the Son of God. Perhaps this knowledge helped Him to stand up to everything.

And after the Resurrection, why didn't He show himself to more people than the friends that had left Him and denounced Him when He most needed them? Did He blame Judas for His death? Did He think less of Thomas because he would not believe in the Resurrection until he had seen Him with his own eyes? As no ordinary man, He would be able to forgive them and the people who kept making war. At least, they said, He forgave everyone just like God would.

But people will always be enemies, because people will always have different opinions. Without differing opinions, the world would be a dull place to live in.

Then the bell went, bringing him back to the lesson. He was usually the first out. 'I enjoyed that,' he said to his friend.

'You must be kidding! Soon we'll be able to repeat every word he says.'

'But I wasn't listening, I was thinking.'

(Susan)

18. Suffering

When Sally came to the hospital over two years ago, she was a normal child, except for one thing, she had an incurable disease. Today she is dead.

She never failed to raise a smile or do what she could to help anybody. In fact, she was a perfect patient.

But gradually the disease crept over her, the first effect being that her body became so thin that she looked like a child of four or five instead of eleven, as was her age. When her mother came to visit her though, she was very happy and they chatted together for the whole of the visiting time. Her illness never affected her mentally, as her mind was still very active.

The next 'stage' of her disease was that, because she was so thin, her limbs could no longer support her. They became so weak that she had to crawl around – as she could not even stand. This condition deteriorated even further so that every few feet she crawled, she collapsed, and had to push herself with her maximum effort back on to her knees and elbows. It was a pitiful sight, and everyone did everything they could to help her – but it was useless. In fact we had to put her in bed and she had to lay there all day.

We could do nothing for her except make her as comfortable as possible. But three months after she was confined to bed she lost the use of her limbs altogether and she had to be fed and every thing done for her. Three months later she died – about two and a half years after being admitted to hospital.

I had often wished she had died to release her from the terrible physical pain and suffering she had endured. But throughout her illness she was very active mentally although her body had badly deteriorated.

(Wendy)

19. Crucifixion

Three wooden crosses stood in the centre of a noisy crowd, most of whom had gathered to witness the execution of the blasphemous Jew, Jesus of Nazareth, who was now nailed to the central cross between two murderers. Inside his brain he was experiencing a more fierce battle than that of his body which was wracked with pain.

'God, God! Must I feel such pain? Is it necessary for me to be crucified? Answer me! Answer me and give me strength to endure this.

These people mock me while I suffer so that they might be saved from an eternal torture.

Oh! My hands burn me as if Satan's darts were piercing them. Help me God!

These children around me, mocking, laughing, but I suppose that if I want them to have a chance to redeem themselves I must suffer the torture that they would have me endure. My happiness will be in Heaven, I must believe this.

Soon God will be down on a winged chariot to carry me, his son, up to the Kingdom.

The pain worsens. I can't endure it much longer. Yet I must not cry out and give in!'

At this point his tortured body could endure no more.

'My God, My God, why hast thou forsaken me?'

Then his lifeless head dropped limply upon his shoulders.

(Timothy)

20. Thy Brothers Hath Returned

'Time scale base in oscillating pattern at three mica climax.'

'Course plotted and ready.'

'Final check correct – am sending – now.'

The capsule glowed, bathing the launch room in raw orange radiation and then dissolved instantly, leaving only burning images in shielded retinas.

The time had come and a myth was to be solved, man was going back.

In the dark cool evening sky the capsule appeared and accelerated away to the east. Man and animals scattered as the fiery glowing demon shrieked over and above, cutting its way through the still night. It curved earthwards and, hovering on tall air columns, lowered itself gently to the ground.

A hatch opened and three tall graceful figures emerged, jumping softly to the ground, unhampered in their light flexible armour, silver in the half moon.

They turned as one and walked softly, warily, across the arid landscape towards the dark city faintly twinkling in the distance.

Three pairs of eyes showed dimly through the multiple visors, eyes set with mission; this was the climax of all their training, just a few more miles. As they trudged towards the city, their suits working to get rid of their free running sweat, they could hear faint but distinct sounds of celebration, of feasts and drunken frenzies; they were on time.

Unhitching their automatic rifles they walked towards the city gates where the sentry, hearing their approach, merrily lifted his eyes trying to see through his drunken stupor. His eyes focussed and he fell back in terror at the tall silver devils who approached him. They passed by seemingly ignoring him, as he, forcing his paralysed limbs to move fled in blind terror to the big wooded city gates. The leader stepping forward raised his rifle and, in a shower of burnt wood and flame, proceeded calmly to cut a large hole in the gates, using his weapon's vicious stream of bullets as a saw. Inside the gates soldiers came running and stood, weapons ready, to attack the monster that must be destroying the gates. A large section of the gate, the cutting completed, tottered and fell inwards. The three figures ran in and, as a few spears hit their suits with useless thuds, raising their automatic weapons cut the soldiers up and into oblivion with the odd twitching limb, with the efficiency of the guillotine.

They ran on, using their murderous weapons only when challenged, until the hill was before them, its three ominous shapes, shadows against the night.

The crowds had gone and the few left ran away to hide in the lower gardens.

The three men stopped uncertainly and looked upwards – it was so real, as humanists had imagined it. In the receding twilight they saw the crude wooden spars with that man hung limp on them, the brown dirt streaked nakedness of his body, his long graceful limbs now crippled and cruelly impaled on stake ripped by his own weight, the head hanging forward with its long flowing hair streaked with blood from his head wounds, his eyes closed, his chest shallow moving. Life was going. They would have to be quick.

Two of the men ran to the base of the cross and started erecting some portable climbing frame.

The one who remained slowly reached up and undoing its clasp lifted his helmet and threw it away into the night. The moon breaking the clouds showed his long silken hair, the high cheek bones and dark eyes which now brimmed with silent tears that ran down over his pale drawn cheeks.

The other man signalled him to help them and puzzled at his inaction.

He shook his head.

'We are wrong. We are wrong,' he whispered and slowly he began to raise his lowered weapon. One of the other men looked up in surprise and reached for his weapon in a frantic lunge. The angry roar of the automatic broke the night air. The man, his suit split wide open, spun away, his body in bloody ruin, to collapse a shapeless heap. The other man reached his feet before his head and shoulder were ripped away, his torso tottering, to fall against the cross and slowly slipped to the ground.

The man on the cross, slowly, painfully, opened his eyes and lifting his head looked down.

Their eyes met but there was no understanding.

The weapon slipped from unknowing fingers and he turned and walked slowly down the hill towards the gathering soldiers; he could hear the man's strange cries behind him getting gradually fainter.

(Charles)

Epilogue

I would like to use this epilogue to make it quite clear to the reader that I have written the opening sections of this book as a personal manifesto and not an impersonal treatise, as polemic, not detached analysis. Polemic comes from the Greek word πόλεμος meaning war, and it has been my aim to attack much of our present secondary system of education and some of the wider social pressures which have brought it into existence. In the manner of polemic I have tried to keep the attack simple, direct and incisive. Dewey claimed, 'The statement of aim is a matter of emphasis at a given time.'[51] There is no point in emphasizing those things which we have already achieved in education but there is a real point in emphasizing the many needs and defects which, simply because they exist, teachers tend to accept as inevitable shortcomings.

It has also been my aim, not only to attack our present secondary education but to suggest an alternative to it. While I have presented this alternative in my own way, I claim no originality for its content. Philosophers as diverse as Plato, Rousseau and Dewey have all insisted that a real education has to be based on experience, either real or imaginative, and must involve the whole person. 'Avoid compulsion,' Plato said, 'And let your lessons take the form of play.'[52] In the 30's A. S. Neill, Susan Isaacs[53] and many others demonstrated the soundness of Plato's prescription. And today, nearly all our nursery schools and a large number of our primary schools are run both happily and effectively on such principles. Again, it has been my aim to present this view of education as simply and directly as possible.

What are the chances of this viewpoint being adopted in our secondary schools? It is depressing that Risinghill[54] in London and Braehead[55] in Scotland – two secondary schools which courageously endeavoured to link learning to the delight of experience – were closed down for 'administrative reasons'. It is depressing that there is a tendency among imaginative teachers to leave the secondary schools in order to find work where their gifts are more readily appreciated. It is depressing also to watch the power and number of examinations growing. Over 100 years ago, Matthew Arnold, in one of his many reports warning people against a tendency to rely too much on mechanical processes and too little on intelligence, claimed that the teachers would abuse examinations by making them the self-justifying goals of their efforts. 'In the game of mechanical contrivances,' he wrote, 'the teachers will in the end beat us.'[56] How prophetic Arnold's words have proved to be.*

Yet there is some room for hope. At either end of the secondary school, in the primary school and in the university, a revolution in education is under way. If the student revolution extends down into the sixth form of the secondary school and the revolution in the primary school moves upward into the first and second forms then it is likely that we will achieve a continuous and enlightened system of education.

It is of particular interest here that the revolution now taking place in the primary school was, in many ways, sketched out in the 1931 Report on Primary Schools. I would like to quote at some length from this report as it also summarizes the main claims I have made in this book for the secondary school:

> ... The principle which is here described will be challenged by no one who has grasped the idea that life is process of growth in which there are successive stages, each with its own specific characters and needs. No good can come from teaching children things that have no immediate value for them ... We must recognize the uselessness and the danger of seeking to inculcate what Professor Whitehead calls inert ideas – that is, ideas which at the time when they are imparted have no bearing upon a child's natural activities of mind or body and do nothing to illuminate or guide his experience.
>   ... [The curriculum] appeals less to passive obedience and more to the sympathy, social spirit and imagination of the children, relies less on mass instruction, and more on the encouragement of individual and group work, and treats the school in short, not as the antithesis of life, but as its complement and commentary ...[57]

These recommendations were made nearly forty years ago! Why has it taken the primary schools so long to put them into practice? Certainly one of the main reasons was the 11 plus which the report, absurdly, insisted on. As long as there was to be an external selective examination, as long as the criteria for judgement remained outside the actual process of education, as long as there was a concern for results (good results for the pupils, the parents, the teachers, the headmasters) and hence, success, so long did the ideas that connected education with living seem idealistic, impractical – even dangerous. Yet the moment

---

* The only hopeful sign in the immediate present is the way in which a number of schools are considering completely dropping the G.C.E. examination system where the syllabus is imposed and adopting mode 3 C.S.E. in which each Department can create its own course for its own pupils.[58]

the 11 plus disappeared – or showed signs of so doing – it was these very ideas that poured into the schools and proved themselves to be not only practical but infinitely superior to the traditional 'sit still and learn' approaches.

If one studies a recent Educational Report, 'The Middle Years', one can begin to see how the methods now being used in many of our primary schools might extend into the secondary schools. The age-range of the report is interesting – 8–13 – because it connects the last three years of the primary school with the first two years of the secondary school. The report states:

> Nowadays we allow children to proceed at their own rate, whether they are using an arithmetic test or working with materials. To do this, the timetable is divided into blocks of time rather than individual lessons. Some teachers have found this arrangement sufficiently unsatisfactory to allow even these limits to be broken: children proceed with a piece of work until they have come to a satisfactory conclusion. This may take half an hour, all morning or a whole day. This pattern demands a high degree of organization of materials, media and the teacher's time. Once such organization is established it is possible to proceed to a situation in which children freely choose their work from activities available. The class timetable disappears, apart from a few items when the whole class may be using a facility which is shared with the rest of the school. Each child works out his own timetable . . .'[59]

Such a school clearly bases itself on the living experience of each individual child. The tragedy is that three years after the individual leaves such a school, he will be expected to sit external examinations with imposed syllabuses. To do this, he will have to cover at the depth or superficiality required, what the Examination Board demands him to know. And the more he wants success, the more he will have to adapt himself to the pressures of the system. The Report on the Middle Years shows a definite dissatisfaction with the way examinations affect the secondary schools. Dr G. Matthews, organizer of the Nuffield Foundation Mathematics Project, after claiming that the central message of the New Mathematics is 'Let the children think', goes on to say:

> The only serious message that I have is 'End Exams.' This is the only way of cutting the knot . . . It can be done. It has been done in Canada. It has been done in America.[60]

It is, it seems, a choice between personal education and mass competition, which, as I have argued in the book, is ultimately a choice between love and hate, between being and having. No wonder that the contemporary debate on education is so intense: the very nature of our society is in question.

The student movement, although this may not yet be realized, is in many ways a natural extension of the revolution in the primary schools. One of the fundamental complaints made by students is that the universities, while they claim to be centres of culture, imagination and reason, are often little more than places where unreal specialisms are taught, where learning and experience are severed, where individuals are trained in order to fit back into the unquestioned divisions of the existing society. Certainly it would seem true that whereas students in the past were content to speculate about social change, or study it as a subject, students today are committed to bringing it about. Understanding, freedom and experience, they assert, must run together. And this, surely, in a different context, is very much like the philosophy behind the revolution in primary schools.

At the end of their study of the student revolution in France, Patrick Seale and Maureen McConville conclude:

> The Gaullist state may be strong, but, no more than any other society, does it really know where it is going or how its community will tomorrow be organized. For a decade, perhaps even much longer, the French have not asked themselves fundamental questions about the nature of their society. They have allowed it to be shaped, often inhumanely, by the scramble to modernize, industrialize, become competitive . . .
> . . . There was a more hopeful side to the May Revolution. A torrent of critical energy was released which, for a moment, made officialdom cringe and left every emperor naked. It carried the germ of hope that the intellect, the spirit and the imagination, if given free range and scope, could really change the world.[61]

And the May revolution is beginning to have its effects on French education. The Ministry of Education has issued a circular urging that marks should be abolished for most forms. At Vincennes, a new experimental university has been opened:

> By French standards the organization of the university was to be highly unconventional. In official language it was to have a mission of 'pluridisciplines' intended to produce 'multidimensional' men. The curriculum . . . and the actual administration was to be left entirely to the teachers and the students to work out . . . Academic progress will be charted by a system of continuous notation.[62]

Of course, these changes may well be pretences at reform by the Gaullist régime – nevertheless, in time, such reforms, whatever their political motivation, are destined to chart new directions for society.

In our own universities students are being granted more freedom to regulate their studies and more powers to participate in administrative decisions. It is interesting too that many departments are experimenting with more flexible examinations, while others have moved completely over to continuous assessment. It cannot be long before the spirit of change in the universities spreads to the secondary schools. As soon as universities give up examination qualifications as their means of selecting sixth-formers and ask for work to be submitted and teachers' individual reports, as soon the mystique of passing examinations will end. And then, the many new approaches (now thought to be 'interesting theory') will pour into the secondary schools as they did into the primary schools the moment the 11 plus disappeared. When this happens we will have achieved, for the first time, a continuous education committed to the fulfilment of man as man.

In *Has Man a Future?* Bertrand Russell claims:

> One of the troubles of our age is that habits of thought cannot change as quickly as techniques, with the result that, as skill increases, wisdom fades.[63]

It should be the specific task of modern education, not only to impart the complex variety of techniques that support a technological society but also to develop those qualities of being, love, sensitivity, understanding, imagination, which ought to determine the uses to which such powerful techniques are put. No thinking or feeling person can over-estimate the urgency of this task.

References

1. 'The Report on Primary Schools, 1931', quoted in *Education Documents*, edited by Stuart Maclure (Chapman & Hall) p. 189. (My italics.)
2. Jules Henry: *Culture Against Man*. (Tavistock Publications) p. 292.
3. Peter Abelard: 'Sic and Non', quoted in *The Age of Faith*. (Time-Life Books) p. 95.
4. Oxford Board. G.C.E. 'O' level, Summer 1968.
5. Søren Kierkegaard: *Concluding Unscientific Postscript*. (Princeton University Press) p. 317
6. *Primary Education*. Editorial. 8th January 1965.
7. John Vaizey: *Education for Tomorrow*. (Penguin) p. 23.
8. R. H. Tawney: *The Acquisitive Society*. (Fontana) p. 190.
9. R. D. Laing: *The Politics of Experience*. (Penguin) p. 87.
10. Martin Buber: *Between Man and Man*. (Fontana Paperback) p. 25.
11. John MacMurray: *Persons in Relation*. (Faber and Faber) p. 60.
12. Martin Buber: *Between Man and Man*. pp. 27–8.
13. Erich Fromm: *The Art of Loving*. (Unwin Paperback) p. 94.
14. Einstein: *The World as I see It*. (The Thinker's Library) p. 5.
15. Edwin Muir: *An Autobiography*. (The Hogarth Press) p. 42.
16. See A. S. Neill: *Summerhill*. (Penguin).
17. See *The Story of a School*. (H.M.S.O. Education Pamphlet No. 14).
18. See Sybil Marshall: *An Experiment in Education*. (Cambridge University Press).
19. R. D. Laing: *The Politics of Experience*. (Penguin) p. 49.
20. For an extensive study of the use of language in different social classes, see Basil Bernstein's: 'Social Class and Linguistic Development' (reprinted in *Education Economy and Society*, ed. Halsey, Floud and Anderson).
21. Here is a commentary by John and Elizabeth Newson on attitudes to the body revealed by parents of four-year-olds in Nottingham:

Difficulties are especially likely to occur, of course, in houses which have no bathroom; the mother may well choose the daytime when the older members of the family are out, as the only time in which she can secure enough privacy to wash all over; and if she feels that modesty is necessary before her pre-school children this will certainly curtail her freedom of activity. 'If he comes in, I don't stand myself out for a show,' said a foreman's wife. 'I'd use a bit more discretion, kind of thing; I don't believe in shutting him out':

not many mothers could be so firm as the bricklayer's wife who said that, because her little boy had laughed about 'Mummy standing in her petticoat', she would 'always send them out in the yard and always bolt the door and have a wash down, and never let them see a thing – never.' These feelings are closely linked to social class; indeed, the correlation is striking (see table below).

	I & II	IIIwc	IIIman	IV	V	All random
	%	%	%	%	%	%
1. Child may see both parents	59	45	27	24	15	32
2. May see only like-sexed parent	22	23	22	22	17	22
3. Child may see neither parent	19	32	51	54	69	46

(The Newsons classify the subjects of their interviews by the father's occupation. Classes I & II are professional and managerial; Class IIIwc, white collar; Class III, skilled manual; Class IV, semi-skilled; Class V, unskilled.) See *The Four Year Old in an Urban Community* by John and Elizabeth Newson (Allen and Unwin).

22. See for instance: *Discrimination and Popular Culture*, ed. Denys Thompson (Penguin); *Magazines Teenagers Read* by Connie Alderson (Pergamon); 'Mass Civilization and Minority Culture', by F. R. Leavis in *Education and the University* (Chatto & Windus) and the works of Raymond Williams and Richard Hoggart.

23. Osip Mandelsam quoted in *The Sunday Times*: 'Success before Six', 17th March 1968.

24. The *Sunday Times*: 10th, 17th and 24th March 1968.

25. D. H. Lawrence: Why the Novel Matters in *Selected Literary Criticism*. (Heinemann) p. 102.

26. Marshall McLuhan: *The Medium is the Massage*. (Penguin) p. 18.

27. Picasso: quoted by Geoffrey Keynes in his introduction to Blake's paintings, p. 3. (The Masters, series 6. Knowledge Publications).

28. Emily Dickinson, *Selected Poems of Emily Dickinson*, ed. James Reeves (Heinemann) p. 39.

29. Keats – letter to Reynolds, 3rd May 1818.

30. Melville: *Hawthorne and his Mosses*. Stories, Letters & Poems. (Dell Paperback) pp. 43–4.

31. Melville: Letter to E. Duyckinck. 3rd March 1849. Ibid., p. 357.

32. Keats – letter to George and Georgina Keats, April 1819.

33. Keats – letter to Woodhouse, 27th October 1818.

34. Keats – letter to Haydon, 11th May 1817.

35. Braque: from an article in *The Observer*, 1st December 1957.

36. Elizabeth Barrett Browning, 1845, *Preface to Poems*.

37. Sartre, *What is Literature?* trs. B. Frechtman (London) pp. 160–5.

38. Emily Dickinson, *Selected Poems of Emily Dickinson,* ed. James Reeves (Heinemann) p. 75.
39. Emily Dickinson, *Letters of Emily Dickinson,* edited by M. L. Todd, New York and London, 1931.
40. Emily Dickinson, *Selected Poems of Emily Dickinson,* ed. Conrad Aiken, (Jonathan Cape) p. 106.
41. Ezra Pound: *A.B.C. of Reading.* (Faber Paperback) p. 28.
42. Ibid, p. 32.
43. Paul Valery: quoted in Arthur Koestler's *The Act of Creation.* p. 317.
44. Edmund Leach: Fifth Reith Lecture, 'A Runaway World'. (B.B.C.)
45. Amy Lowell: *The Creative Process.* (Mentor Paperbacks) p. 112.
46. Good examples of books which have helped to discredit the traditional methods are: Holbrook's *English for Maturity* and *English for the Rejected* (Cambridge University Press), Clegg's *The Excitement of Writing* (Chatto and Windus), and Shepherd and Poole *Impact Teacher's Book* (Heinemann Educational Books).
47. Roland Cahen: *Problems in Psycho-Analysis.* (Burns & Oates) p. 107.
48. Anne Sexton: *The New Poetry,* ed. A. Alvarez. (Penguin) p. 59.
49. Ted Walker. Ibid., p. 225.
50. R. S. Thomas, Ibid., p. 80.
51. John Dewey: *Education and Democracy* (Macmillan) pp. 111–12.
52. Plato: *The Republic* VII. 536.
53. See Susan Isaacs: *Intellectual Growth of Young Children,* and *Social Development of Young Children.* (Routledge and Kegan Paul).
54. See Leila Berg's: *Risinghill.* (Penguin).
55. See R. MacKenzie's: *The Sins of the Children, Escape from the Classroom,* and *A Question of Living.* (Collins).
56. Matthew Arnold 'General Report for 1867', quoted in *Educational Documents,* p. 81.
57. *Primary School Report, 1931.* Ibid., pp. 189–92.
58. See Robin Guthrie's 'How Progressive Can a State School Be?' *New Society.* 6th February 1969.
59. *The Middle Years of Schooling.* (Working Paper no. 22 . H.M.S.O.) pp. 68–9.
60. *The Middle Years of Schooling,* p. 65.
61. Patrick Seale & Maureen McConville: *French Revolution 1968.* (Heinemann/Penguin) p. 229.
62. Peter Lennon: 'Ferment in French Education', *The Guardian,* 18th January 1969.
63. Bertrand Russell: *Has Man a Future?* (Penguin) p. 9.